MANIFESTING GOD'S LOVE

—— *through* ——

SIGNS, WONDERS,

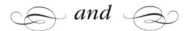 *and*

MIRACLES

MANIFESTING GOD'S LOVE

through

SIGNS, WONDERS,

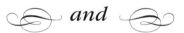 *and*

MIRACLES

Jerame Nelson

DESTINY IMAGE® PUBLISHERS, INC.

P.O. Box 310, Shippensburg, PA 17257-0310

"Speaking to the Purposes of God for This Generation and for the Generations to Come."

This book and all other Destiny Image, Revival Press, MercyPlace, Fresh Bread, Destiny Image Fiction, and Treasure House books are available at Christian bookstores and distributors worldwide.

For a U.S. bookstore nearest you, call 1-800-722-6774.

For more information on foreign distributors, call 717-532-3040.

Or reach us on the Internet: www.destinyimage.com.

Trade Paper ISBN 978-0-7684-3291-6

Hardcover ISBN 978-0-7684-3489-7

Large Print ISBN 978-0-7684-3490-3

Ebook ISBN 978-0-7684-9077-0

For Worldwide Distribution, Printed in the U.S.A.

1 2 3 4 5 6 7 8 9 10 11 / 14 13 12 11 10

ENDORSEMENTS

I love this book! From the first pages, I was drawn by the stories and insights that Jerame shares. It encourages me that a young man has pressed into Father God and come away with such life-changing wisdom. The keys that Jerame shares will open doors for you!

Steve Long
Senior Pastor, Catch the Fire Toronto
(formerly Toronto Airport Christian Fellowship)
Toronto, Canada

In this generation, God is raising up new voices with a fresh spirit of faith upon their lives who dare to take the Body of Christ into places we've never been before. Jerame Nelson is one of these new voices. I have known both Jerame and Miranda for several years now and have directly experienced the substance of Heaven that they carry on their lives. By reading this book you will experience no less. Jerame is called to break the Body of Christ into something fresh, and in this book, he reveals Kingdom keys that release fresh insights into divine encounters with the Living God, calling the generations to arise and take hold of their unique destiny. Enjoy!

Jeff Jansen
Founder of Global Fire Ministries
GFM World Miracle Center
Murfreesboro, Tennessee
Author of *Glory Rising, Walking in the Realm of Creative Miracles, Signs and Wonders*

Love is the key we must all possess, and when we turn this key, power is released! Even small keys can open big doors; that's why a smile or kind word can sometimes be the greatest sign or wonder. *Manifesting God's Love* will show you how you can both possess this key and turn it as well.

Rick Pino
Fire Rain Ministries

Jerame's book is packed full of refreshing insight and perspective. I love the theme of being equipped with intimacy, authority, and revelation which are some of the main keys to living a successful life. Jerame shares out of his own prophetic journey and uses examples of how he is on track with the very message of the book: manifesting love through the power of God. To all those who don't just want another book on signs and wonders but are ready to be unlocked to be the sign and wonder, read this and follow in Jerame's footsteps. Then as understanding gets unlocked in you, let this book prophesy to you so that you can help to be one who unlocks this generation just like Jerame!

Shawn Bolz
Senior Pastor of Expression58
Author of *Keys to Heaven's Economy*, and *The Throne Room Company*

Jerame is a young man who carries the DNA of "a new breed" that God is raising up to carry the message of the Kingdom with signs, wonders, and miracles. Over the years that I have known Jerame, he has grown in maturity and integrity, and this book reflects the journey he's been on. I strongly suggest that you read this book. It will inspire as well as launch you into walking in the supernatural power of God.

Trevor Baker
Senior Leader
Revival Fires Ministries
Dudley, UK

Will you be one who possesses the keys to Kingdom power and revelation and unlocks the sacred door to unleash a revolution of love?

TABLE OF CONTENTS

FOREWORD

It is a joy to write the foreword for Jerame Nelson's new book. I have enjoyed getting to know Jerame over the past four years as we have traveled and ministered together many times in different nations of the world. You will be thrilled by the testimonies of God's healings and miraculous power, as well as by the supernatural stories he shares in this book. This book is an invitation to know God more as well as experience His great love through encountering Him in supernatural ways. We are living in a time when God wants us as a Church to live naturally supernatural. God wants to restore to us the same power and visitations that we see the early church in the Book of Acts walking in. The supernatural was a commonplace thing in the first-century church. They were used to seeing the manifestation of God's power through signs, wonders, and miracles, as well as encountering Him in supernatural dreams, visions, and angelic encounters.

In the Book of Acts chapter 12, you have the story of how Herod was persecuting the church and killed James, the brother of John. Herod then also arrested

Peter to kill him. When this happened, the Bible says that continual prayer was offered up to God on Peter's behalf by the church (see Acts 12:5). As God heard their cry, He sent an angel to Peter to rescue him from the hand of Herod. Peter then fled to Mary's house where many were gathered to pray for him. As he knocked on the gate to the house, a servant girl named Rhoda came to the gate and recognized Peter's voice. She ran back into the house and told those who were praying that God had answered their prayers and that Peter was at the gate. Instead of having faith that God had answered their prayers, the church told the servant girl Rhoda, *"You are beside yourself...It is just his angel"* (Acts 12:15). When they finally realized that God really had answered their prayers and released Peter from prison, they were astonished. The way the early church acted in this event seems to be a very strange way of behaving and thinking. They had more faith that it was Peter's angel standing at the door than they did that God heard their prayers and released Peter from prison. What is that all about?

I believe that the early church was used to the supernatural. They were used to seeing angels and having supernatural encounters with God. I believe that God is restoring the supernatural to the Church. This book is full of supernatural encounters that completely line up with the Word of God. I believe that your life will be changed by the truths found in this book. Jerame does an amazing job of giving you keys to walking in the supernatural in everyday life, as well as to positioning yourself to live a lifestyle of manifesting God's love through signs, wonders, and miracles. Not only do I endorse Jerame's book, but I also fully support all that he and his precious wife Miranda are doing to advance the Kingdom of God.

Bobby Conner
Eagles View Ministries

INTRODUCTION

Ever since I gave my life to Jesus, I've lived with one desire—to know Him and to live in the revelation that He brings. Out of my relationship with God, I've had so many supernatural encounters with Him and within His Kingdom here on earth that I am excited to share with you both the amazing variety of supernatural experiences that I've had and the keys that I have been given. They are keys to knowing Jesus.

They are keys that He wants you to have, too.

Specifically, in this book, I want to release three main keys to you—keys to intimacy, authority, and revelation. Each one unlocks a corresponding door—the doors to intimacy, authority, and revelation. As we unlock these doors, we will see that Jesus is leading us someplace specific...into the inner courts of His counsel where He tells us what is to come.

And I am going to tell you what is to come, because you are invited. In fact, this book is one long invitation to join those of us who want to launch a revolution of love in the world—a love revealed through signs, wonders, and miracles.

First, you need to make the supernatural encounters of revelation part of your experience. They are not just for me or a handful of others. God is calling you to come up higher! He wants you to experience Him—with a revelatory knowledge, not just an intellectual knowledge.

This book will help you know more about how to access the keys and unlock the doors to revelatory encounters. Read on and see that there are some things that you can do to obtain the Kingdom and release the manifest presence and manifest revelations of God's love to a lost and hungry world.

Let's go beyond the initial stage of meeting God and move into your destiny in this hour. He wants you to move into ongoing encounters with His love, His manifest presence, and the Holy Spirit. And He invites you to move with Him to release Heaven on earth through miracles, signs, and wonders. This invitation is for anyone who will receive it.

Something *big* is coming.

Will you accept the invitation?

CHAPTER 1

SEARCHING FOR THE KEYS TO THE KINGDOM

Jesus unlocked the doors of Heaven and revealed an unsurpassed authority, power, and revelation to men, and even now, He is holding out the keys to His Kingdom and inviting you to release His glory on earth. It is as if He is pointing to you and saying, "There's one that's faithful. There's one that I can anoint. There is one I want to release My keys to that will unlock the doors to the authority and power of Heaven. Will you accept My keys? Will you come and gather them from the deep places of intimacy with Me? And reach out for them on the high places of My kingdom? Then turn the lock in the door and unleash a revolution that the world longs to see? A revolution of My love?"

I sought to possess these keys that would manifest God's love to the world through signs, wonders, and miracles—and the Lord was faithful to answer. In a moment in time, He revealed three specific keys that I will tell you about in this chapter. They include the key of David (the key that releases authority), the key of revelation knowledge (that releases power), and the key of love (that releases God's presence and launches a revolution). They are the keys that open the doors to the abundance of the anointing.

There are other keys I will tell you about in this book as you read. They are keys God wants you to possess as well.

He's looking for those who will just be radically in love with Him and obedient to the things He said and taught when He was in the earth. He is looking for those who are hungry to be like His disciples and to seek after Him, asking, "Lord, what are the keys? Lord, how can I walk in the same love, authority, and power You did—as the man Jesus Christ?"

Let me tell you how they came into my possession. I happened to be in Fort Mill, South Carolina, speaking at a conference during Yom Kippur with Rick Joyner and remembered that Bob Jones, a well-known prophet, had prophesied to me the year before about a coming visitation. He said, "You need to wait on God on Yom Kippur, 'cause He'll visit you and give you the word of the Lord."

That Sunday, on Yom Kippur, at the most random time ever, in the most "unspiritual" place ever, while waiting on the Lord with a latte in hand, I had a visitation.

I was at Starbucks with a good friend of mine; we had just gotten a latte and gone out to sit in his Jeep to listen to some worship music. We're kicking back, eyes closed, and as we're worshiping God, I suddenly feel the presence of God become really, really strong. And I'm thinking, *Whoa. What's goin' on?*

I open my eyes and see an angel standing outside of the car looking in at me. The next thing you know the angel takes his hand and puts it through the window glass of the car. I'm sitting in the passenger seat watching his hand go through the window; in the angel's hand is a key ring and two keys. One key distinctly reads, "Matthew 16:19." The other key bears the imprint of "Isaiah 22:22." Then audibly the angel says, "It's all about Matthew 16 in this season."

Then, BOOM! he vanishes.

I felt kind of overwhelmed by this. After a moment, I told my buddy, "We've gotta get a Bible, man. I gotta see what Matthew 16 is."

He busts out his iPhone, looks up Matthew 16, and hands me the phone. Then I began to read the passage in Matthew 16:13-19 where Jesus asks His disciples, *"Who do men say that I am?"*

And they reply, "Well, some say, 'Elijah.' Some say, 'Jeremiah.' Some say, 'The prophets of old.'"

He asks them again, *"But who do you say that I am?"*

Then Peter speaks up, "Well, You're the Christ. The Son of the living God."

Jesus replies, "Blessed are you, Simon Bar-Jonah, for flesh and blood has not revealed this to you, but My Father who's in Heaven. He's given this to you. Upon this revelation, you shall be called Peter, or Rock." He continues, "Upon this rock I shall build My church, and the gates of hell shall not prevail against it. And I'll give you the keys of heaven, and whatever you bind on earth will be bound in heaven. And whatever you loose on the earth will be loosed in heaven" (see Matt. 16:17-19).

What do you do with that? I took it back to Bob. But his explanation was even more mysterious than I could have imagined. Since I was in Fort Mill, South

Carolina, the Lord worked it out so we could hang out with Bob and his wife Bonnie the next night. Bob, being a prophet who has had years of revelatory encounters with heavenly beings, explained the encounter to me. He said, "That wasn't just an angel that visited you. That was the 'Wisdom of the Ages.'" He said, "The Wisdom of the Ages visited you."

The wisdom of the ages is contained in those scriptural passages passed along to me that day.

God wants to release wisdom to us in this hour so that we can begin to tap into everything God has for us and release something that was uncreated into existence—a fresh move of God's love and power onto the earth. He's after a people who know who they are in Christ, and know who Christ is inside of them. He's after a people who don't just *talk* about their God, but *know* their God. And as the Book of Daniel says, they do great exploits for Him (see Dan. 11:32).

God is going to release keys to us as a Church to begin to walk in apostolic and governmental authority, and He's going to allow us to see and to taste that He is beyond good—He is love.

The Key of David

Let's take a look at these keys in Scripture and see what they can do as you step out and use them. The first key the angel revealed is the key of David written about in Isaiah 22:22.

Isaiah 22:22-23 states,

> *The key of the house of David I will lay on his shoulder; So he shall open, and no one shall shut; and he shall shut, and no one shall open.*

> *I will fasten him as a peg in a secure place,*
> *and he will become a glorious throne to his*
> *father's house.*

God wants to unlock things to us in the Spirit that no man can open.

I really believe that this is going to be the year of the open door, and that God is opening up things for us as a Church that we've not yet been able to enter into. We're on the brink of seeing one of the most powerful moves of God, a revolution of His love, in the United States. But here's the deal. I believe it's going to come through the people of God. It's going to come through the saints doing the work of the ministry because God is raising up an army in this season. It's not just going to be about the apostles, prophets, evangelists, pastors, and teachers doing everything while everybody watches. See, the Bible says that those giftings are given to equip the Church for the work of the ministry (see Eph. 4:11-12).

Get ready, saints. Jesus is handing you the keys. And He's asking you to begin to walk in the authority of the Kingdom of God so that when you begin to pray, prophesy, and speak the word of God, signs will confirm that word, and wonders will happen. All over the world I believe we're seeing a shift in which more authority will be released to the remnant in the Church, the ones who are His friends, the ones who know their God and are going to do great exploits for Him.

I love how God confirms to us that He did indeed send an angel or release a visitation. After almost every experience I've had, God either shortly does what He said He would do to or through me in a meeting, or He confirms the encounter.

One week after this visitation where the angel gave me the keys on Yom Kippur, I was preaching in New

Jersey about the keys. Afterward I joined some others in the back room to eat dinner, and a pastor from Maine walked up to me. He said, "Hey, I'm kind of freaked that you preached on the keys of the Kingdom from Isaiah 22:22. God told me to bring this with me to the meetings, and it is one of my most prized possessions."

He held out a key and explained, "It's a key of David that Chuck Pierce gave me. Two years ago Chuck traveled all around the United States with Dutch Sheets, declaring the message of Isaiah 22:22, and he gave one governmental key out to one specific leader in every state in America. He also gave one of the keys to President Bush. I didn't know why I was supposed to bring this, but when I heard you speaking, the Lord spoke to me, and He said, 'I want you to give that key to Jerame Nelson because he's to have it for this next season.'"

Chuck Pierce and Dutch Sheets had gone around prophesying about the key of David, said that it would bring breakthrough in the nation, and handed this man the key to Maine—a key that Chuck Pierce prophesied over specifically. The pastor went on to tell me that Chuck prophesied that this key would be a special key that would affect the entire nation; it would affect all 50 states, and it would even go all around the world.

I love how God confirms His word when He is speaking. One week after I had the visitation, I received the Maine key of David for the United States of America. I believe this is a token sign of where we are at in the Body of Christ right now, and I believe it's a sign that God wants to open doors that no one can shut and close doors that no one can open.

Now I want you to understand something: there are several keys the Lord showed me He wanted to release that had to do with governmental authority. One of those keys is the key of finances; if we are going to do what God is calling us to do as a Church, we must have the finances of Heaven.

I believe that it is God's intent to provide for His people who are focused on doing Kingdom things. Some of you have not yet stepped into your dreams; you have not yet stepped into the mission field, or into things that God had promised you because you have not had the finances. You're focused on the Kingdom but need a breakthrough in the area of finances. Breakthrough is going to happen as you walk into a kingly authority and anointing. The change that occurs in you will manifest into the "change" you need in your pocket. The key of David enables us to walk in that kingly anointing and draw prosperity, the material things you need to build the Kingdom. Let's take a look at this key.

Kingly Authority

The kings, or the prime ministers, who ruled during biblical days, wore on their royal garments a key sewn onto their shoulder. The key signified that they were the governing authority over the entire land. What they said had to be obeyed. If the ruler would gesture "Yes," to a question or decision that needed to be made, that gesture meant that the door was open, and nobody could shut it. But when he said, "No," that meant that the door was completely closed, and nobody could open it.[1]

The key was not something that needed doors; the king's *word* opened or shut the door. I am not talking about possessing a physical key, but a kingly authority, a royal authority from Heaven. God wants His kings to rise up and His lords to take their place on the earth and in America. A lord is someone who owns land, an occupier of land. How many know that God wants us, as His people, to take back what the devil has stolen from us and from God? We have the keys to the Kingdom on our shoulders, and He wants us to use them.

We need an authority that goes beyond just what we say and what we pray. We need power to be demonstrated when we begin to speak the word of God. When we begin to prophesy, we want that word to come to pass.

Like Samuel, God wants to put an anointing upon us so that when we speak the words of God there is life on them, and those words don't fall to the ground. They come to pass, and people begin to listen to the Church. This is going to be a year when God restores His voice to the Church. Some of you might say, "How does He restore His voice?" We will have a voice when God restores His supernatural power and begins to release His glory—when the goodness of the Lord is seen.

When the darkness creeps in and rears up to bring fear upon the land, that's when we as sons and daughters of the living King begin to stand up with the authority that He's given us. We begin to take dominion and reverse the spread of darkness and fear by first using the key of David.

Let me give you an example of using the key in your own hometown.

Just recently, my wife and I moved to California. In this state, we're seeing people lose their homes like crazy. We're seeing businesses fail, and there is an even greater shaking that's happening. But I believe God is allowing this shaking to happen to position the Church to begin to take dominion. May the darkest hour of the world become the Church's finest hour. I believe as we begin to understand spiritual laws and principles found in God's Word, we will begin to step into a place of breakthrough. You see, it was out of a place of intimacy and obedience to God's voice that we moved to California. When we came onto the scene in San Diego, even though the economy was not doing well and many people were having a hard time, we stepped into the favor of the Lord. We received an incredible deal on our home and moved into a place that we would not have been able to afford in a normal economy. We ended up getting our home for 50 percent off of its original price. God worked an amazing miracle for us because we were operating out of the key of intimacy when we moved. He said to move there; we heard His voice and obeyed, and the Lord broke open the way for us—financially and spiritually.

The government of God should be resting upon the shoulders of kings. God wants to challenge us to know that we are kings and queens in our own hometowns. And as we step into positions of spiritual and governmental authority in our communities, God will release us to worldwide prominence and expand our territories. He will take you places that you never dreamed to unlock the heavens and release His presence and power on earth.

Accessing the Key of David

David was a lover of God—the key that he wielded was the key of intimacy with God. Many of you have been in a place with Him in intimacy. Some of you feel hidden. This will be the year that some of you walk through the doors of destiny. While you've felt hidden, and nobody's noticed or recognized you, God's been doing a work in His fire. Now He's going to reveal you in this season. God's going to open doors, and He's going to shut doors. The key of David will loose for us what God has already loosed in Heaven on our behalf, and it will also bind the things that God has already bound in Heaven.

When we operate in that key of intimacy, break-through will happen. Intimacy releases breakthrough. And it's not going to require waiting for ten years to see it happen. It's going to be *now*. We're seeing a "now" breakthrough, people getting miracles of healing more quickly than ever before, regional strongholds being broken, and nations turning to the Lord.

Jesus *is* the key of David. Let's look at Isaiah 9, and you'll see what I'm talking about:

> *For unto us a Child is born, unto us a Son is given; and the government shall be upon His shoulder. And His name will be called Wonderful, Counselor, Mighty God, Everlasting Father, Prince of Peace. Of the increase of His government and peace, there will be no end, upon the throne of David and over His kingdom, to order it and establish it with judgment and justice from that time forward, even forever. The zeal of the Lord of hosts will perform this* (Isaiah 9:6-7).

Jesus came to the earth for a purpose: to seek and save that which was lost (see Luke 19:10). So many of us get confused because we've got a lot of evangelists running around saying that Jesus came to seek and save those who are lost. That's not what the Word says. It says Jesus came to seek and save *"that which was lost."* In this verse, Jesus was talking about the authority that Adam lost in the Garden when he sinned.

He's talking about the mandate of dominion rule and reign in the earth that the devil snatched up when Adam fell in the Garden. Jesus is the one who opened all the doors that needed to be opened and shut all the doors that needed to be shut when He died and rose from the dead. On that day when He asked who men said that He was, Jesus proclaimed to Peter, "I am getting the keys back, and I'm giving them to you. I'm giving you those keys so that wherever you go, you can bind and loose whatever the Father shows you and whatever He speaks to you. Do what He says when He says to do it. If you will declare what He says, then, what He says will happen."

We access the key when we access Jesus. Knowing Jesus as a friend who is closer than a brother releases a co-laboring partnership empowered through intimacy. And that intimate relationship with Jesus releases to us the key of revelation and knowledge that will transform nations.

The Key of Revelation Knowledge Transforms Regions and Nations

How do we begin to step into a place of accessing Isaiah 22:22? I believe that we have got to come into a place of revelation knowledge. In Luke 11:42-52, Jesus rebukes the scribes and Pharisees for all the different things they were doing that were legalistic and religious.

Luke 11:52 tells us about a key—the key of knowledge. If we are going to operate with the key of David, which is the governmental authority of God, then we need another key, the key of revelation knowledge, to enable us to see into what God the Father is doing and hear what He is saying. That key draws us into greater intimacy with Jesus and empowers us to stand up against not just the demonic principalities and powers, but the religious spirit that still exists in Christian circles. Luke 11:52 says, *"Woe to you lawyers! For you have taken away the key of knowledge. You did not enter in yourselves, and those who were entering in you hindered."*

Jesus was bringing a rebuke to the religious leaders of His day because they opposed having true relationship with God in the Spirit. They would rather follow legalistic traditions and practices of man than have real relationship with God. They hindered people from seeing and hearing from God. Religious people are not bothered when we read the Word or say a little prayer, but the minute that power starts to show up, or we see an angel, or God gives us a dream or vision, or we begin to take ground in the spirit, that's when religious people say, "I don't know if this is of God."

The religious mind-set seeks to stop people from accessing the key of knowledge and the key of intimacy. If we are going to do something for God in this season and in this hour, we have to have this key.

This key is the key of John 5:19; Jesus said He did nothing but what He saw His Father doing. John 5:30 says, *"I can of Myself do nothing. As I hear, I judge: and My judgment is righteous, because I do not seek My own will but the will of the Father who sent Me."* I believe that when we begin to step into this kind of anointing, we will see both the government and the power of God.

We can begin to move with the authority Elijah exhibited when he walked up to the King Ahab and said, "Yeah, look. There will be no rain but by my word." And drought happened (see 1 Kings 17:1). What is this but governmental authority in the Body of Christ? Elijah also rebuked the false prophets of his day. Challenging them at Mount Carmel, he saw an entire backslidden generation come to the Lord in one day.

Is God's arm too short to do it again? I don't think so. What would happen if we went right up to the White

House and said, "Hey, you know what? There will be no rain in this land until you overturn Roe vs. Wade!" I'm telling you, they'd laugh at you at first. But if the rain stopped, they'd take you pretty serious. God has another way of dealing with things, but it's higher than our ways, and it's supernatural.

One day when I was in Alberta, Canada, I was waiting on the Lord, asking Him what He wanted me to do in the next meeting I was scheduled to speak in. And the Lord told me to use the key of revelation and knowledge in a dream.

First, this song came to me in a dream, and the lyrics were something like this: "I'm releasing a Spirit of Elijah, purity and intimacy across this land."

If the religious spirit had hindered me, I would only have preached about purity and badgered people into cleaning up their lives. But revelation and knowledge cause us to do only what we see and hear Jesus doing. So it was a no-brainer what I was to preach, right? Elijah. I stood up and preached about Elijah and the key to authority through intimacy with Christ. When I got to the end of the meeting, much to my surprise, the Lord told me, "I don't want you to move in miracles because I want to prove to these people that I am God; I want to confirm My word."

He then told me, "Decree the key that I gave you. Decree the release of the Spirit of Elijah."

So I decreed it at the end, and then He prompted me to sing the song I heard in my dream. Very simply, I just sang the song of the Lord over the people and region; I decreed that God was releasing the spirit of purity and Elijah.

Then the Lord said, "Now get the church to call fire down on the prophets of Baal!"

We all started singing, "Lord, release Your fire."

After we sang about the fire coming down, they closed the meetings. Several of us went out to lunch. Within a half hour of our declaration in the natural, we heard about a hotel in the city overtaken by drug dealers, pimps, and prostitutes that supernaturally caught on fire during the time of our declarations and singing. It burnt to the ground. No one was killed, but the stronghold of lust and perversion was destroyed that day in that city. This was a sign in the natural of something that God did in the heavenlies.

I believe that this is the way the Church must operate if we are going to see breakthrough in this nation. We must get strategic keys and decrees from God the Father; and as we begin to decree them, breakthrough will happen. When we went to lunch that day, we weren't aware of what had happened. It's not so much about knowing the results as it is about obeying what we hear and releasing the heart of God. As we begin to tap into the heart of God, I'm telling you, that's when breakthrough happens.

Intimacy with Jesus develops in us the ability to trust that we are hearing Him correctly. Our relationship with Him invites us to move into His ways and demonstrate the power of the keys—locally and globally.

Demonstrating the Power of the Keys

My wife Miranda and I have a ministry to Indonesia and are seeing Muslims saved on a regular basis. We are going into the darkest places where nobody wants to go. One of the hotels I stayed at two years ago just got blown up. We know God is with us, and if God is with us, who can be against us? We know the risk, but we go.

Recently, we were in a city called Manado where we stepped into a series of experiences where we could see the power of the keys released through our lives in greater measure than ever before. We had no idea what to expect but just stepped out in faith when God told us to go and work with a certain man we had met in a meeting in Indonesia. When we met, the Holy Spirit said to my spirit, "Work with this guy; he's a really good guy. Go with him." And so we went with Pastor Frans and watched God open doors that no man could shut.

I'm telling you: if you just listen to the voice of God, you'll prosper.

When we got to Manado, we were shocked! I was expecting to do a church service for maybe 500 people. When I showed up, I discovered that a $450,000 crusade was paid for—a stage, lights, cameras, and a crowd of 6,000 to 7,000 Muslims waiting for God. I thought, *Wow, this isn't what I thought I was coming for.*

But this is what they told me, "Jerame, we are hoping that you guys can make a difference here because you are a healing ministry. Here's the deal: we put on these crusades, and we've tried to do this stuff, but we have not had much breakthrough, especially with the young people. No young people ever get saved, and we've got all these street kids coming 'cause we feed them. They said they are here to listen to the music and stuff, and we are hoping that maybe you guys can reach them."

You know what I did? I went home right before this meeting, and I said, "God, I need a strategic key. How are we going to bring a breakthrough for this meeting?" I'm not afraid of a challenge. We shouldn't be. So I said, "OK, Lord. What are we going to do?"

The Lord began to show me how to release the strategic key of knowledge. I was already using the key of David—authority and intimacy. I now needed to release the key of revelation knowledge that would release power.

You see, God wants us to position ourselves to begin to receive this key of revelation knowledge. You position yourself by saying, "Lord, what are You doing? God, what do You want me to do? How do You want me to pray for that person at work? Lord, who do You want me to buy lunch for this week?" I'm sitting there in Indonesia, and I ask, "Lord, what do You want me to do about this?"

The Lord replied, "Jerame, the Muslims will listen to you if you demonstrate My power." He said, "I want you to guarantee that the first five deaf people that come onto the platform will be instantly healed—or I am not God."

That's what He told me to tell them.

I said, "OK, God. Fine. I'll do it." I've developed that absolute trust in Him because I've heard His voice so many times. You have to get to the place where you can honestly say, "God, I'll look like a fool for You." I had already flown all the way over there. Might as well.

I got up on the platform during the crusade and said, "I'm not going to preach at you guys. The first five deaf people who come on the platform will be healed. I guarantee it, or my God's not really real."

You know what happened? Exactly five deaf people came out of the crowd of six thousand, and they lined them up in front of me. One by one, we began to pray. One ear opened. Two ears opened. Three ears opened. Four ears opened. And then I got to the fifth one, a little girl about seven years old who had never heard a sound in her right ear in her entire life. She was deaf because she had no ear canal, no middle or inner ear. Only a flap of skin on the side of her face resembled an outer ear. I said under my breath, "All right, God, You'd better show up." I prayed for her. When I took my hand off that little ear flap, I saw she had received a brand-new ear canal and likely, the inner mechanics of a brand-new ear because she could now hear.

When that happened, do you want to know what it did to this place? It came unglued. Miracles started to break out. People in a wheelchair section who had been crippled for years began to jump out of their wheelchairs and run. People who had tumors, deaf ears, and blind eyes started getting healed—without anyone even praying for them.

That night revival broke out. There were over six hundred young Muslim kids on the ground at the front of the altar weeping and writhing like snakes and being delivered from demons. It was the biggest harvest that they had ever seen in this city. The key of revelation knowledge opened the doors to those miracles and unleashed the government—the rule and reign—of God.

When the Kingdom shows up, it attracts attention. Those miracles also opened the doors to the government on earth. When I woke up the next morning, I received a phone call from a man who said that the governor of the entire province had heard about the miracles and wanted to know if I would come and preach the Gospel to him. I asked, "God, what do You want me to do?"

The Lord said, "I want you to preach the Gospel to them. I want you to preach Isaiah 60."

When you ask God what to say, when to say it, and how to say it, when you position yourself not to do things out of your own flesh, but out of the leading of the Holy Ghost—you're accessing the key of revelation knowledge. When you do what He says, that governmental, kingly anointing comes to bring it to pass—that's kingly anointing.

When I got up there, I opened up the Bible to Isaiah 60. I declared that the glory of the Lord was going to be seen in this land even though it was very dark. I prophesied that God was going to draw people from all around the world. They would come to that place because of the natural glory that was there. Then I began to prophesy Isaiah 60:5-6 where it says that the wealth of the Gentiles will come to you. When I looked at the governor, I could see that the Word was touching him; praise God.

At the end of it, the governor came up to me, and he was visibly shaking. Through the translator, he said, "Thank you."

After the governor left, his right-hand guy came to me and said that I had really freaked him out. He explained, "He knows that your God's real because you prophesied everything that's happening here in a few month's time, even though we know that you don't know that; that's what really hit him."

Apparently, the governor was only planning on being there to shake my hand, but his aide said to me that there was this strange presence that arrested him; he could not leave. The governor interpreted the word according to what they had been building in the natural. Two months after I gave this word, they were going to have what's called The World's Ocean Conference; for two years they had been building new highways and hotels. They were expecting millions and millions of dollars and hundreds of thousands of people from around the world to come at that time, and it did happen. The wealth of the Gentiles came to the natural glory that was there—for the best scuba diving in the world and for the conference.

When I prophesied that, the governor was open to hear the rest of the word. At the end of that prophecy, I began to declare all kinds of different things about government; I told them that they needed a government founded on the Gospel of the Kingdom of God. Since then, the governor has been filled with the Holy Ghost, and he's saved.

It was wonderful to release the keys of authority, power, and revelation knowledge during my time in Indonesia. But there is one more, all-important key to access and release. This key ensures that what you say and do remains in the hearts of those who are touched by your ministry. You can have all power, but if you have not love, it is meaningless. Love tears down strongholds not only in a person's mind—but over whole regions.

The Key of Love

The most important key in this hour is the key of love.

God is about to release a love revolution to the Body of Christ. I want to define what it is to have a revolution because I believe that God wants to bring real language to the Body of Christ so that we understand what He's doing in this hour. I believe we're about to enter into a heartfelt revelation of love that is greater than God's power and greater than His gifts.

A revolution is not reformation. A revolution is a drastic and far-reaching change in ways of thinking and behaving that will affect cultures. A revolution is also defined as the overthrow of a government by those who are governed.[2]

It is time for you to step through the doors of the Kingdom into the revolution of God's love for you. It is time for you to grab hold of the keys that will change your way of thinking and unlock the doors to intimacy, revelation, and power. Do you want to be part of the new revolution? God is calling you.

The Key

The key of David speaks about developing a relationship with Jesus that opens the door to Heaven's revelation. The key is intimacy. Intimacy with Jesus develops in us the ability to trust that we are hearing Him correctly. Out of our relationship with Him we hear Him inviting us to move into His ways and demonstrate the power of the keys—locally and globally.

Opening the Door

Lord Jesus, come and release to me a greater ability to draw closer to You, to really know You, and to hear only Your voice directing me during this day. Teach me to hear Your voice. Attune my ear to hear the words that You are personally speaking to me every morning. And as I go through my day, come with me. Make me mindful of Your presence. Talk to me about Your love for me and for others. Enable me to love You with my whole heart, mind, and soul…and reveal Your heart of love through me to others…even today.

Endnotes

1. www.cgom.org/Publications/MiniStudy/
    MS-TheKeyOfDavid.pdf.

2. *Merriam-Webster's Collegiate Dictionary,*
    11th ed., s.v., "Revolution," (Springfield, MA:
    Merriam-Webster, Incorporated, 2004).

CHAPTER 2

GATHERING THE KEYS
OTHERS POSSESS

If you want to be part of the revolution—not just a spectator, but one who rushes in and takes the Kingdom—you need to possess the keys I am talking about in this book. The only way you can possess them is if you want them badly enough. And if you want them badly enough, you must reach out and grab hold of them. Gather the keys I offer in this book. Then search around and gather the keys others possess.

From the moment I met the Lord, I started learning from others about Jesus and the ultimate plan of the universe: to experience God's love and give it away. Love, power, and revelation unlock the doors to the hearts of men and women and open them up to receiving Jesus as their Savior. Learning from others was central to me becoming a disciple. However, I also knew that the Holy Spirit is the ultimate teacher and that I needed to learn to walk in the counsel and might of the Lord.

I remember when I first started learning from God how to walk in the counsel and might of God—I stumbled across it by accident. I had read Isaiah 11:2 that talks about the seven Spirits of God; right away, I said, "God, I want to walk in the counsel and might of God." I didn't even know what I was talking about. Honestly.

Then one night God graciously gave me a dream. During this time in my life, I was playing baseball at Sonoma State University, and I had really long, curly hair. In this dream, my mom comes in with these hair clippers in her hand and she's running at me with clippers like she is trying to cut my hair off. I'm trying to hold her back, saying, "What is this?" Then I wake up, and I'm talking out loud, saying, "I rebuke you, devil. You aren't cutting my hair off."

But right away, the Lord spoke to me. "Jerame, you said you'd follow My counsel. Why don't you go get a haircut?"

And I said, "God, are you serious? What do you mean, go get my hair cut? I like my hair."

And He replied, "You don't even care what you look like."

That's what God told me. So I said, "Alright."

At the time of the dream, I was in Colorado visiting my family on a Thanksgiving break. So I told my mom, "I gotta go get a haircut." She decided to come with me and get her own hair done the same afternoon.

I was thinking, *This is just like my dream,* as we went to a hair salon called Cost Cutters, one of those low-end design places where I thought *there is no such thing as getting the latest style.* They put a bowl on your head and go "brrrrr," and when you look in the mirror, you're like, "Man, what happened to me?" So I walked in, and I'm sitting there in the foyer, kind of nervous about what I'll end up looking like. Then a woman called me to come back. She started washing my hair, and in the process of making small talk, she asked me a dangerous question: "So what do you do for a living?"

What I live for is to witness for Jesus. That's it. If I can find a doorway to do it, I'm going to do it. So I told her, "I'm a missionary." For some reason, I decided not to tell her I was playing baseball and had only been on one mission trip in my entire life.

"Really!" she said. "So you like to build houses?"

"Not exactly."

"What do you mean, 'Not exactly?'"

I said, "I believe in Jesus. And I believe He's the same yesterday as He is today and forever, and He does miracles."

"Really. That's kinda funny that you're saying that. In fact, this is my first time on the job in a year and a half."

"Really?"

"Yep. I've been in the hospital."

At this point, I was starting to think, *OK. I've been set up.*

"Yeah, for a year and a half I've had congestive heart failure and blood clots up and down my legs, and the doctors have been unable to do anything for me."

It was the open door I needed. I said, "Well, hey, you know what? When I was in India on this mission trip, we saw blind eyes and deaf ears opened, people getting healed out of wheelchairs. God's power is real."

The woman was shocked and stopped washing my hair for a moment. Then she said, "I've never heard of a Jesus like that."

That's sad. We need to start opening our big mouths and letting what God has put in us come out. So I started telling her testimonies about the healings I had seen recently. By then her faith and understanding had been built up, and I said, "Before I leave, I want to pray for you."

And she said, "OK."

She sat me down in another chair, started cutting my hair, and by the time she was halfway done with the haircut, she had heard a few testimonies of miracles that I've seen. To be honest with you, at that point, I hadn't seen that many. I told her three or four that I had seen in India, and then I started telling of other people's miracles. Suddenly, right in the middle of the haircut as I'm telling her these testimonies, she stopped.

She said, "You're not going to believe this."

"Believe what? My hair's gone?"

"No, seriously. Ever since you began to tell me about these miracles, this heat has come onto my body. What's crazy is for the first time in a year and a half, all the pain in my legs is gone."

I was thinking, *Praise God!* I didn't even lay hands on her. The next miracle I'm seeing is this: "God, You're really right. I look better with short hair."

I continued to minister to the woman and said, "God doesn't want you halfway healed. He wants you fully healed. Let me pray for you." Right there in the middle of Cost Cutters, full of people, including my mom who is getting her hair permed, I just prayed, "Father, release Your fire."

And she said, "*Oooh!* It's hot in here." She started sweating.

"That's Jesus. He's got a fiery love for you."

Right when I thought nothing could get better, the lady who was perming my mom's hair said, "I need a miracle in my body too."

I asked her, "What's wrong with you?"

"Well, my kidneys have been infected, both of them, for about three months now," she said. "I've been to three doctors. It's so bad I can't even use the restroom without excruciating pain."

"Well, let's pray for you." She was healed on the spot!

Two miracles were released in the middle of Cost Cutters. One woman got saved. And it all happened because I followed the counsel of God, which simply told me to "go get a haircut."

Knowing the counsel and might of the Lord involves spending time with Jesus, getting closer to Him. So close that you have an ongoing intimacy with God that leads you to trust His voice. Then obedience to His voice will release the manifestation of His glory and the supernatural. God wants us to walk in manifest power. He wants us to walk in the supernatural. I'm telling you right now if you hear His voice say to do it, you have all authority in Heaven and earth to see amazing things happen to you and through you.

Following the Lord's counsel implies that you are listening—both to Him and to others. If you want to soar in the supernatural, you need to be open to learning, to having a teachable spirit. Don't miss out on the times of glory that are coming your way.

Learning From Forerunners

Jesus was a man who walked in the supernatural. Jesus walked on water. He walked through walls. When an angry mob grabbed Him by the scruff of His neck to throw Him off a cliff, He disappeared and walked right through them (see Luke 4:28-30). He walked in the mystical realms of Heaven on earth. He was a forerunner who revealed that we, too, will do greater works than these (see John 14:12).

We have the spirit of counsel and might. We also have many forerunners who possess the keys to unlocking the authority, power, and love that will transform the world. God wants us to reclaim that supernatural ability. Others have. So can you.

Lest you think that we cannot do the same things Jesus did when He walked the earth in bodily form, the Bible cites other examples of those who stepped out in the spirit of counsel and might and transcended the natural laws as they walked into the spiritual atmosphere. The Bible contains another example of someone who walked on water (see Matt. 14:29).

Matthew 14:25-30 says that all of Jesus' disciples were in a boat. He had told them to go to the other side, and He would meet them there. They thought He would either catch another boat or walk the long way around and catch up to them in a day or two. So when He walked up to them on the water later on, they all freaked out. They thought He was a ghost. And then when He revealed Himself to them, Peter said, "Lord, if it's You, tell me to walk on the water to You."

You know what happened. Jesus said, "Come." And Peter took His hand, got out of the boat, and walked on the water.

If God speaks it to you, you have authority to do it. If we will begin to be obedient to God, the manifestation of the supernatural will happen. I believe that Peter stumbled upon a principle in the spirit that governs walking in the supernatural. The reason why Peter was able to walk on the water is because Jesus said to do it. The supernatural is always released by the leading of His voice. I've had many supernatural experiences with the Lord, and every single time they've happened, they've been initiated by some act of faith and obedience on my part. Fortunately, I find my faith level raised up by those who have stepped out in faith long before I was born. I've watched and learned from them. And it makes it easier for me to hear and obey.

When we see God raise up people who walk in supernatural experiences, power, and authority, we need to glean from them. We need to be in tune with a simple prayer: "God, what are the keys that you've given them so that I can have them?"

Gathering the Keys Our Forerunners Possess

I got where I'm at today because I've not only learned from biblical forerunners but also from many fathers and mothers who taught me in the spirit by their example.

I not only watched them and listened to them, I began to ask questions. You know what I did when I was a young intern traveling around the nation with different people? I would go to the meetings and sit on the front row, and I'd ask one particular question, "God, there's a key of the Kingdom this person possesses. Lord, what gold nugget have you given them? Lord, show me the nugget of gold that you've given them."

Being open to the answer enabled me to see different aspects of the Kingdom in different people. And I would say, "Alright, I'm going to take that and make it my own." All of a sudden, I saw the impact of receiving their impartation. I've been maturing in Christ, and the Lord's given us a worldwide ministry. It started with me gathering the keys others possess and saying, "You know what, God? I want the Kingdom. I want the reality of the Kingdom. I want the keys to the Kingdom so we can manifest the glory."

God wants us to have teachable hearts; when we go places, we don't go to receive the manifestations. We go to receive the revelation. The manifestations happen because He's here. It's the revelation that will change you.

Jesus' disciples were so hungry to see what He saw that they pressed in even though they didn't get the same results. They went to cast a demon out of the boy who had a spirit that seized him and threw him down into the fire, and it didn't work. But they didn't let that stop their faith. They saw Jesus pray for blind Bartimaeus and watched as his eyes opened. They saw Jesus rebuke the deaf and dumb spirit. They saw Jesus pray for the lepers. And you know what they did? They didn't just go, "Wow, Jesus!" They came to Him and said, "Lord, teach us how to pray." They said, "God, how are You doing these things? Lord, teach us how to pray. How do You move in this authority? How do You move in this power?"

Jesus responded to their requests. He began to give them the keys. He began to give them the understanding, the revelation. He said, *"In this manner, therefore, pray: 'Our Father in Heaven, hallowed be Thy name. Thy kingdom come. Thy will be done on the earth, as it is in heaven'"* (Matt. 6:9-10).

God wants us to understand that the Gospel is a simple message. Jesus said this: "The key to My power is that when I pray, I believe that Heaven will come to the earth." And He's saying, "This is what sons and daughters do. They walk in right standing with God. And when they pray, they believe that their Father in Heaven is good. And they believe that His perfect will is that Heaven would come to earth and manifest its reality right where we're at."

I often challenge people: if we were to go to Heaven right now, what would it be like? The joy of the Lord—joy unspeakable, full of glory? Angels would be there, worshiping the King. The King of Glory would be there. The presence of the Spirit of God would be there. I mean it would be amazing if we went right now. Now consider what would not be there. Would there be sickness in Heaven? Would there be disease in Heaven? Would there be fear, torment, poverty, and all these things that are capturing the hearts and minds of people in the earth today? There wouldn't. Would there?

If you have a relationship with God—a spirit-to-Spirit contact relationship with Him—wherever you go you have the opportunity, the ability, or the potential to release that Kingdom into this earth so that it touches people. And when it touches people's lives, they're changed forever.

Wherever we go, we see lives transformed—especially while doing street evangelism. I've ministered to atheists, witches, and others who are totally not living for God; those who are initially anti Christ melt in the power of the Lord. We've seen God just wreck people because of the Kingdom. Wreck them with His love.

One time when I was in Vancouver, I took a group of interns with me to the streets, and we were outside of a Starbucks, just sitting there. I felt like God told me to buy a latte and wait right there. I was pretty happy; I had my latte, you know. It's a good day already. Right after I finished drinking it, I thought, "All right, I guess I missed God. I'm not seeing anything happen here." Suddenly a guy wheeled up on his bicycle and said to me, "Hey, man. Do ya got any drugs?"

"No, man. I'm sorry."

And he said, "Are you a cop? Are you an undercover cop?"

"No, I'm not a cop."

He said the strangest thing: "Oh. You're a Christian, aren't you?"

I thought, *Who's evangelizing who?* So I told him the truth: "I'm the prophetic evangelist; how come you're telling me what I'm doing? I don't have any drugs, man, but I've got something better. It's the presence of God. It's Jesus."

"Jesus? Yeah. I tried that before. That stuff ain't real."

"Dude. Jesus is so real, man. I'm tellin' you He loves you. How about you let me pray for you?"

And do you know what the guy did? He gave me a courtesy acknowledgment; he bowed his head and closed his eyes and said, "Oh. Whatever, man. Go." It was almost like, "Come on. Get it over with."

So I was praying, and the interns got the shaba train going—speaking in tongues. They're like, "Shabada-babaka." You know. And the guy probably thought we were really weird.

Anyway, I was praying with him, and I heard the Holy Spirit say, "Jerame, I want you to just release the presence of God. He doesn't need your words."

So I waved my hand past the guy and released the presence of God on him. And he went, "*Uuuhhhhh!* I've been struck," like he was stunned. He jerked up quickly with his eyes as big as saucers and said, "What the heck is happening? I can't believe this is happening. You guys are freaking me out, man!"

He tried to leave and get back on his bike. But when he got on, he was stumbling around drunk, trying to ride down the street. There were like a thousand people on Robson Street, and he wasn't even able to ride his bike in a straight line he was so drunk in the Holy Ghost.

We yelled after him, "Hey! Jesus loves you!" We didn't lead him to the Lord, but we definitely knew that he had an encounter with the Kingdom of Heaven, and he'll never be the same. He mocked Jesus, and he got smacked like Paul. God wants to use us to bring God encounters to people and to release the reality of His Kingdom. The result is up to the Holy Spirit. We may not see it, but we know that we play a part in bringing heavenly encounters to earth.

Walking in the Spirit of Counsel and Might

I believe the Spirit of counsel and might is what God wants to release to our generation because it gives God glory when we see miracles at Starbucks, when we see souls coming in. You know there's a dying, lost generation out there, and they're a "show-me" generation.

We are not living in a time when people want to just hear the Word—they want to *see* something. Why do you think there are guys like David Blaine drawing so much attention to themselves? Why do you think all these TV programs of the reality of the supernatural are so popular? We need to give the "show-me generation" the real deal. And I believe that's going to happen when we begin to walk in the counsel and might of God.

What's the counsel of God? The Counsel of God is the inward secrets of the Lord. It's also the ablility to tap into the blueprints of Heaven by hearing the voice of God. The word counsel in the Hebrew literally means "to receive the purposes or plans of God to execute the purposes of God."[1] The counsel of the Lord works hand-in-hand with the power of God. When you have the counsel of God and the might of God linked together as in Isaiah 22, you have the linking of the raw faith and the raw power of God.

First, let us look at the counsel of God; then we will look at the might.

One aspect of the counsel of God relates to our ability to hear God's voice. His voice can come to us in many different forms: in a dream or vision, an angelic encounter, or maybe even the audible voice of God. For example, Elijah heard God in His *"still small voice"* (1 Kings 19:11-12). Scripture says that when the Lord passed by Elijah there was a mighty wind, then an earthquake, and then a fire, but He wasn't in any of those manifestations. Instead the Lord revealed Himself to Elijah *"after the fire in a still small voice."* God is raising up a generation of friends who love the person of God more than just the manifestations, a people of His presence with the ability to hear His still small voice. Another example of someone hearing the counsel of God's voice is Joseph, the father of Jesus. He heard the counsel of God through an angelic visitation in a dream. In Matthew 2:13 it says *"Now when they had departed, behold, an angel of the Lord appeared to Joseph in a dream, saying, "Arise, take the young Child and His mother, flee to Egypt, and stay there until I bring you word; for Herod will seek the young Child to destroy Him."* Because of

Joseph's obedience to God's counsel in this dream, Jesus was saved from the plans of the enemy. When we listen to God's counsel, we will prosper in all things as well as avoid the plans and attacks of the enemy. Sometimes the counsel of God comes to reveal and protect us from the attacks of the enemy. The key to seeing the miraculous and the defeat of the enemy's kingdom is intimacy with God and obedience to his voice or counsel. It will always result in the power of God being displayed over the devil.

The Spirit of might is the raw power of God. One of my favorite examples of the Spirit of might resting on a man is in the life of Samson. Samson operated in the Spirit of might frequently. The Bible says that when the Lord's Spirit came mightily upon him, he tore a young lion apart (see Judg. 14:6). This is also a picture of what happens when we rely on the strength that God gives. We tear the devil apart. The Bible says the devil walks about like a roaring lion seeking whom he may devour (see 1 Pet. 5:8). It does not say he is a roaring lion. It says he walks about *like* a roaring lion. When we come into a place of the counsel and might of God, the devil becomes exactly who he is—a baby lion.

Another example of the Spirit of might resting on a man is the apostle Peter. In Acts 5:15 we see that the sick were taken out to the streets (on beds and couches) in the hope that if the shadow of Peter passed over them, they would be healed!

So the key to the working of the Spirit of counsel and might is intimacy with God and obedience to His voice. That will release the manifestation of the Spirit and power of God. I can prove it to you out of the life of Jesus.

Jesus and the Spirit of Counsel and Might

When Jesus went to the pool of Bethesda, He only healed one particular man who had an infirmity for thirty-eight years (see John 5:1-15). Have you ever wondered why He only healed this one man, when previously He had healed all whom He came in contact with? I believe the answer lies in verses 17 and 19. Jesus told the Jews who were persecuting Him for healing this man on the Sabbath, *"My Father has been working until now, and I have been working….the Son can do nothing of Himself, but what He sees the Father do; for whatever He does, the Son also does in like manner"* (John 5:17,19).

What I believe happened was that the Father showed Jesus that He wanted to heal the man at the pool of Bethesda in a vision, probably while Jesus was spending time with Him in prayer earlier that day. Then, when Jesus saw the man that He had seen the Father heal (in His vision), He partnered with God by praying for the man. As a result, the Spirit of might was released, and the miracle happened (see John 5:9). The Spirit of counsel and might always releases true authority, and the Spirit of counsel always releases the Spirit of might.

One place to find the keys of the Spirit of counsel and might is in the secret place—the place of prayer. The Bible often mentions the fact that Jesus would get alone with the Father. Sometimes He would get up early before the day began and spend time with God. In fact, sometimes He would even spend all night in prayer (see Luke 6:12). I believe that it's in the secret place of the Most High that the counsel and might of God is accessed. God is looking for people of intimacy to partner with to see the miraculous. Many people want to see the power of God manifest but are not willing to seek out the keys and pay the price in prayer. They would rather go to the next conference or read the next healing book to get the anointing instead of just simply spending time with the Lord. The emerging generation will carry a heart for the secret place. They will be a generation who will confront the powers of darkness and show forth the reality of the Kingdom of God.

I remember one meeting in Atlanta, Georgia, when I was preaching at a healing conference. Before the meeting, in prayer, the Lord began to show in a vision what He wanted to do in the meetings. He revealed that I was to tell the people it was going to be a night of "the pool of Bethesda" and to line ten people up on the left side of the auditorium and prophesy destiny over them. Then He told me before I prophesied over the ten, I was to call out a word of knowledge for those with deafness and arthritis and have those people stand on the right side and wait while I prayed for the ten. He told me if I would do this exactly the way He showed me, He would send a healing angel, and there would be a "pool of Bethesda-like atmosphere" of healing in the place that night.

So I did exactly as He said, and I told the people, "There is going to be a pool of Bethesda-like atmosphere in this place tonight." After I finished praying for the ten, I went to pray for the people concerning the words of knowledge on the right. As I did, I laid my hands on the first, and she fell out under the power and was healed. Then the same happened with the second and the third person. When I got to the fourth, I went to lay hands on her, but she moved out of the way, so I asked, "What are you doing?"

She answered, "I am already healed. I stepped into the pool."

Many others had the same thing happen. Suddenly, a woman came running out of the crowd down to the right side of the auditorium and screamed: "I'm healed too! I stepped into the pool!"

That night at least 23 people were instantly set free from arthritis, and more than five were healed from deafness. One man's ear even opened up as God healed another man who was born deaf! It was awesome. This is an example of the Spirit of counsel releasing the might of God. I did exactly what God counseled (and showed) me to do, and it worked. Certainly, God was glorified!

Do you want to be one who moves in the Spirit of counsel and might? God is inviting you, too. The keys are not just mine to hold. I'm giving them to you. And others who have moved in power for years possess keys that are yours for the taking.

I believe that there's an army that's coming that the devil will not be able to stop, and they're going to be just like the mighty men of David. Of David's mighty men, Scripture says that one man, *"chief among the captains,"* slew 800 men at one time (see 2 Sam. 23:8). That is power.

It is a picture of the end-time army of the Lord that's being raised up right now: everywhere they go, they destroy the works of darkness. Out of their relationship with God, they are able to meet the needs of every person they come into contact with who needs a healing, a deliverance, or the touch of the Lord.

Jesus is so good; He wants us all to walk like He did—as ambassadors of His love and glory. Do you know who an ambassador of Christ is? It's a sent one with authority. And how much authority do they have? They have as much authority as the one who sends them. I'm telling you, that's a day we have to be living for. We've got to be living for that.

There was another level of authority that Jesus had that will aid us as we seek to walk in the Spirit of counsel and might. Jesus walked in so much authority that He said very little, but the word He spoke shattered the rule of the enemy oppressing another's life.

If I were to write a book of the prayers that Jesus spoke as He ministered to people, it would be pretty short: "Shut up." "Come out." "Loose." "Go." "Out." That's it.

I wouldn't be able to write something like this: "Lord, if it's Your will." Or a begging prayer, "Please, God." I think that sometimes when Jesus saw a devil, He just gave a look rather than spoke a word, and they shrieked out. Jesus' presence caused them to tremble.

As we gain understanding of the protocol of Heaven and how the things of the Spirit of God work, we can begin to walk in that anointing that causes the demons to tremble.

Do You Want to Possess the Keys to the Kingdom?

I believe right now God is beginning to call and release people. God is going to harvest harvesters in this season—some of you are going to become some of the greatest evangelists that the earth's seen. There could be someone reading this who is called to shake nations. Do you want to know what's going to be the deciding factor? Your desire to be intimate with Jesus, to know His love, to be willing to learn from others, and to walk in the Spirit of counsel and might.

God wants you to release His Kingdom message. You see the Kingdom message is this: where there's sickness, disease, and torment, you release peace, joy, and righteousness. Where people are suffering and in hardship, you have a substance that's not of this world, a peace you carry into that atmosphere of despair that surpasses all understanding. Through your intimacy with God, you release that peace to them, and it changes things. God wants us to be atmosphere changers so that when we walk into a room, we change the spiritual atmosphere of the environment we are in. God is calling us to carry the light of his glory to a dying and lost world so that they can be brought out of great darkness and into his marvelous light.

God is raising up people who know their God and understand the mandate. Jesus' disciples were amazed at Him, weren't they? The guy's walking on water, walking through walls, doing miracles, multiplying food, and manifesting healing. Demons are coming out; people are being saved and touched by the power of God. All these amazing things are happening. The disciples sought after Jesus and longed to do the same things because of some mysterious calling pulling on them. If you feel that same pull, you are called to possess the keys to the Kingdom and step out to release the supernatural Kingdom of Christ onto a desperate land.

If you are coming with us, you're not just enlisting in a spiritual army destined to march along like infantry. Neither are you called to be an ambassador attached to any one country. You are being called to higher places. It is time for you to transcend the natural and even the older, religious interpretations of ministry. It is time for the Spirit of counsel and might to catapult you into the heavens until you begin to soar in the supernatural.

Soaring Into the Supernatural

Not long ago, I fell into a trance on a plane while coming home from a trip to Indonesia. And in this trance-vision I was preaching. And as I was preaching, there was a woman on the left side of the room who was being filled with the anointing of God. She was screaming and hollering, "Oh, the glory is here!" And so I was wise enough to stop preaching and ran over to check it out.

When I ran over there, the Spirit of God came on my body, and I began to soar in the spirit. As I began to be lifted up off the ground, I said to myself, "I'm going to fly in front of all these people." But then I jolted fully alert; the vision over.

I immediately asked the Lord, "What is this?" And the Lord spoke to me.

He said, "Jerame, I'm telling you, just as I released healings and miracles last year, this next move is going to be a move of the supernatural. I am going to begin to raise up the Body to walk in the mystical realms of Heaven, and they're going to begin to see the same things that the Bible depicts."

Following the Lord's counsel implies that you are listening—both to Him and to others. If you want to soar in the supernatural, you need to be open to learning, to having a teachable spirit. Don't miss the portals of revelation that you are about to soar into.

The Key

The key of the Spirit of counsel and might is found only in the secret place—the place of prayer. The Bible often mentions the fact that Jesus would get alone with the Father. Sometimes He would get up early before the day began and spend time with God. In fact, sometimes He would even spend all night in prayer (see Luke 6:12). I believe that it's in the secret place of the Most High that the counsel and might of God is accessed. God is looking for people of intimacy to partner with to see the miraculous. Many people want to see the power of God manifest and run from conference to conference but are not willing to seek out the keys and pay the price in prayer. If you want greater revelation and anointing, you need to find the key to the Spirit of counsel and might.

Opening the Door

God, I want the Kingdom. I want the reality of the Kingdom. I want the keys to the Kingdom so we can manifest the glory. Come and draw near to me as I draw near to You. Release the Spirit of counsel and might to me. Let me hear Your wisdom and direction for any area of my life You are trying to speak to me about. Open my ears to hear You and the eyes of my understanding to perceive. Let me hear Your direction, and I will step out in faith today as You give me Your counsel and the power to carry out Your will.

Endnote

1. Blue Letter Bible. "Dictionary and Word Search for `etsah (Strong's 6098)". Blue Letter Bible. 1996-2010. 18 Apr 2010. < http:// www.blueletterbible.org/lang/ lexicon/lexicon.cfm?

CHAPTER 3

THE KEY TO OPENING PORTALS OF REVELATION

Bobby Conner likes to talk, and unless he's got a big steak in his mouth, there's words coming out. When I travel with him, he often just tells me stories of his experiences during decades of prophetic ministry. While traveling to Holland with him for a ministry trip, it seemed like he told me about every supernatural encounter with God—every time he has been translated or transported someplace, every time an angel visited him, and even every time the devil has visited him. It was awesome!

Right before we got on the plane to head home from that trip, he decided to tell me the reason behind all those stories. "Jerame," he said, "Do you want to know what I've been doing all week?"

"What?" I asked.

"I've been imparting to you. *The testimony of Jesus is the spirit of prophecy*" (Rev. 19:10). Then he continued the lesson. "Hey, Jerame, I want you to understand something. Do you want to walk in the supernatural?"

I said, "Yeah."

"Talk about God," he said. "In the Book of Colossians, it says, if you'll talk about God, if you'll keep your mind fixed on things above where Christ is seated at the right hand of God, then you'll become heavenly minded (see Col. 3:1-2). Then, gates, doors, and portals of Heaven will open, and you'll walk through 'em."

Bobby was handing me the key to soaring in the supernatural, to opening portals of revelation that I could fly right into. And the key is this—talk about the testimony of Jesus, and you will experience more.

I went home with that gift lesson, and the next weekend I flew to New Jersey where I was going to minister with a great friend of mine named Craig Kinsley. I told Craig about what Bobby shared with me. I said, "Craig, dude, I learned some stuff last week with Bobby. I learned that if we'll talk about God, and if we'll be about the things of the Kingdom, heavenly minded, we can step into the doors of the spirit, and we can experience the supernatural."

So I challenged us to talk only about God-stories. "I challenge you to talk about God the entire way home," I said to Craig. "Dude, I challenge you, let's talk about every miracle you've ever seen, every visitation; let's talk about Smith Wigglesworth's, Bob Jones, William Brahnam, Jessie Duplantis; let's talk about anybody that we know who's walked in it and just see what happens." We were flying from New Jersey back to Abbotsford, Canada, on the west coast, so we had plenty of travel time together.

From New Jersey to Toronto, we just started talking about God. Then we switched planes in Toronto and flew to Vancouver—the closest city to Abbotsford. The whole flight, we're talking God-stories. All of a sudden, right in front of our eyes, we started seeing bright flashes of light. As I began to look at these flashes of light, I realized that Heaven was invading the plane, and these flashes of light were angelic beings sent from God. Then, as we were looking at the angelic beings moving all around the plane, we started noticing gold dust falling on us.

It was awesome. And so we kept talking about the amazing life in the spirit and supernatural encounters with God's presence and power and Kingdom invading earth.

Once we arrived in Vancouver, my brother Josh picked us up from the airport. As soon as I got into the car, I said, "Dude, you're not going to believe it. We just started talking about God, being obedient to what we heard as the Word of the Lord to us from Bobby Conner and a challenge to talk only about God stories. And you know what? These angels started manifesting and gold dust started falling in the plane. It was crazy."

We merged onto the highway in Vancouver while we're telling my brother about our recent events, and I glance back at Craig in the back seat just in time to hear him let out a yell of surprise.

"What?" I ask.

And he says, "Dude, we're in Mississippi. What's going on?"

So I look out the car window and much to my shock, I see what he is seeing. We're no longer in Vancouver. We're in some other place. Even my brother who is driving realizes that the road is no longer familiar. It appears that we were instantly and briefly transported 2,700 miles off of one highway to another. Craig, still looking out the window, says that he sees this guy mowing the lawn and recognizes him as a friend that he grew up with in this city. I'm looking around thinking, "Man, this place is weird."

Then all of a sudden, I look back at Craig and, *boom!* we're back on the highway in Vancouver. After Craig got home, within a few days he called his friend in Mississippi and said, "You were out mowing the lawn just a few days ago, weren't you?"

And his friend said yes. Craig was able to describe exactly what his yard looked like.

What was the purpose for this experience? I believe that God is raising up a generation who will live "naturally supernatural." It will be out of a place of intimacy with God and obedience to His voice that they will access the keys to the heavenly realm. Hebrews 13:8 says that God is the same yesterday, today, and forever; He never changes. If God would transport men of old in the Bible such as Elijah, Philip, and even Jesus, why would He not do the same today? I believe that God was showing us what He is capable of showing to His friends. I also believe that God is going to begin to open up Heaven and visit His people. God wants to give you encounters because He wants you to know His heart more and to release His heart to others. God wants to visit you, too. He wants to give you angelic encounters. He wants to give you dreams and visions. If you'll be intimate and obedient with God, and talk about God, keeping the testimony of what He is doing and has done foremost in your awareness, you'll have increasing encounters with God.

Talking About God-Stories Releases Angels and the Winds of Change

One time while ministering in Edmonton, Oklahoma, I was with my friend Craig Kinsley again. For some reason, when we get together, crazy stuff happens. There's a synergy sometimes between people who have a unity of spirit or similar focus in the spirit. That synergy opened up a new dimension of Heaven in a place that seemed resistant to the presence of God.

We were in Edmonton facilitating a revival on Central Oklahoma University's campus, a secular campus. We were meeting in the ballroom of the campus, and we were freaking people out. After all, we were ministering in the religious Bible belt of America where people are used to spirituality packaged in a correct, decent, and orderly way, right? The lady who invited us to come didn't tell us that it was an evangelical church, unfamiliar with manifestations of the Holy Spirit. The first night we got there, I said, "Craig, you're preaching first."

He went out, preached, and it was really, really hard. No one seemed receptive. The next day was my day. I was lying on my bed in my room before the meeting, trying to soak in worship and praying, "I need the word of the Lord for tonight for these young people." As I was soaking, I kind of fell asleep. Then I realized that's not working and decided that I should start praying in tongues. While I was speaking in tongues, my voice started going away. I wasn't sure what to do but knew that I needed to stop speaking out loud to save my voice.

So I sought God for further direction: "Lord, what do I have to do here to release breakthrough?"

And I heard the voice of the Lord say, "Why don't you spin around like a little kid?"

"That's strange. But OK. Why not?"

So I just started spinning around like a child. I spun, and I knew it had to be supernatural because I did it for what seemed to be a full five minutes and didn't throw up. Suddenly, as I'm spinning around, out of Heaven, right in front of my face, an angel appeared.

This was the first time I'd ever had an angelic visitation that clearly. This guy was huge, wearing a white garment with a golden sash; he had long hair and a crown on his head that sported a red jewel. I stopped spinning to stare at him. He just looked at me, glaring with arms folded across his chest.

I mean I was lucky I didn't wet myself right there. I was freaked out. I thought, *What is this?* Then he just disappeared through the roof, and I was left wondering if this just happened.

Something caught my attention on the floor, and as I looked down, I saw a feather about four inches long, curled spirally, like a Christmas tree. I picked it up, and it dawned on me that my obedience pulled an encounter out of Heaven.

The Lord said, "Jerame, if you'll be childlike and do what I say when I say to do it, miraculous things will happen." He added, "Unless you come with the faith like a child you can't see God" (see Matt. 18:3).

Immediately, I went next door and knocked on Craig's room because I knew he was inside, also praying. He opened the door; I held up the feather and said, "Craig, look!"

He grumbled, "That's not fair," then slammed his door. I could hear him in there saying, "God, I'm your son. I want a visitation too." And he started pressing in, praying in tongues as I walked away.

I went back to my room and sat there petting the feather, thanking God that He loves me. You know, when you have encounters with God, they're fun. When you find that a diamond or a feather is dropped at your feet, it brings joy. For a while I just rejoiced that the Lord visited me. Not long into my new prayer time, Craig came into my room, looking shocked and amazed.

"That's the look, dude. You had something happen, didn't you?" I asked.

He nodded his head and said, "Dude, while I was in there crying out, this angel came in. All I could see was the feathers spinning around making kind of a whirring sound. And then he took this branding iron out, and he branded my heart with the Song of Solomon." Craig, too, had a supernatural encounter with God, and I hadn't even told him that I had been spinning.

After we both had these encounters, we did not know what to think about them. What do sons do when they don't know what to do with visitations that God gives to them? I'll tell you what…they call their spiritual fathers. So that was exactly what I did. I got a hold of Bobby Conner and told him all that happened with both Craig and me. Then I asked him what he thought about the angelic visitations we had. He explained to me that it was the Angel of the Winds of Change who had visited both Craig and me.

Later the Lord began to speak to me and give me keys to visitations with Him out of our experiences that day. He said, "Jerame, you've got to hunger for Me." He said, "Craig was desperate, and he made a demand. He saw that I visited you, and he made a demand because he's a son too, so I had to visit him."

What's amazing about angelic stuff is there's always fruit in the aftermath. That night I went to the meeting and preached on the "Double Portion of Elijah." The miracle power of God came into the room so heavily that it was crazy. There was one young girl who had about thirty metal pins and seven metal plates holding her face together because it had been badly injured and broken two years before. When I got a word of knowledge and said, "There's somebody with metal in their body. Come forward," she came forward. When I prayed for her, God melted all of the metal out of her face. Then she testified that for the first time in two years, she could feel the sensation of touch on her face right there on the spot. Later on, her doctors confirmed that all the metal had disappeared and the bone structure had reformed.

As a result of that miracle, faith erupted, and twenty other people were instantly healed. As the Winds of Change began to blow, revival broke out on the campus!

In one of the other meetings while Craig was preaching, there were a couple of football players who had been injured and were sitting out the season. They were instantly healed, crying like babies as God touched them.

Intimacy and Obedience Releases Heaven's Intervention

When you have an encounter with Heaven, God's presence increases. The way to experience more God encounters is through intimacy and obedience. Both Craig and I were in prayer, spending time with our Father, talking to Him, waiting for Him, and expecting that since we are His sons, the Father would want to come and talk to us. That mutual conversation is called relationship. And the more time we spend relating to God, the closer, more intimate we become. Then, we learn to trust that God is speaking to us, and it gets easier to step out in faith and obedience to do what we hear Him saying. Intimacy and obedience release Heaven's intervention.

If we really get the understanding that it's intimacy and obedience that release Heaven on earth, things will happen. God will give you authority over the weather. We've seen moments when God has given us authority over the natural elements, and it's always out of obedience. Let me tell you about one instance.

I was on a plane traveling from Calgary to Abbottsford. The stewards were passing out drinks when the plane suddenly started making some frightening noises as it flew through turbulence, causing people's drinks to spill all over them. The pilot got on the intercom and said, "Hurry! Get the drink carts back. We're going to be in severe turbulence for about twenty minutes. This is an emergency."

Coffee was flying everywhere. We were all getting nervous.

Then the Lord spoke to me. "Jerame, would you do something about it?"

I asked, "What do you mean?"

And He said, "Command it to stop."

I immediately said out loud, with everyone in earshot hearing me, "In the name of Jesus, stop now."

And total peace descended on the plane. Not one more bump occurred the entire way. The Bible says Christ Jesus has set us free from the law of sin and death (see Rom. 8:2). That includes natural laws. If we understand what causes these kinds of manifestations, we will have authority that transcends nature. That authority comes only in relationship and in obedience.

Philippians 2 offers a spiritual principle about how intimacy and obedience works. Look to the interests of others and do nothing out of selfish ambition (see Phil 2:3). It is God who works in you to act according to His will. That means stepping out in obedience—for the sake of others.

If you will just begin to step out and pray for people, miracles will happen. Why? Jesus already gave the commission. He said, "Go into the world and preach the good news of the kingdom of God. And those who have faith in Me," He said, "they'll cast out devils, they'll speak in tongues, and they'll lay their hands on the sick, and they'll recover" (see Mark 16:15-18). Do you know what that means? That means you have a promise from God.

Because you have that promise of His Word, that commission, all of Heaven will back you up if you'll be obedient to it.

My wife takes that commission to heart and doesn't wait for a moment to ask God what His will is. She just knows it and steps out in faith and obedience to the Word. As a result, she is like an evangelistic machine who sees so many miracles everywhere she goes. It's crazy. I can't even take her to the mall without her praying for everyone in sight. That's what we call outreach by the way—shopping. A month and a half ago she showed up for a hair appointment and discovered that the hairdresser just broke her rib. My wife sat down and said, "Oh yeah? Well, you know God's here right now, and He can heal you."

She didn't even pray for her, and the rib went "pop." She was instantly healed. But she found an excuse to go into the back room to check it out and started moving around.

There her coworker noticed her moving and asked, "What's going on? You couldn't do that before."

Later Miranda came back to the hairdresser for a second visit, and when she did, her hairdresser told her that she had an X-ray done after Miranda had prayed for her. The doctors could not find even a sign of a break because the Lord had given her a brand-new rib! That's when her hairdresser began to tell Miranda about the seizures she had been having every day since she was a little girl.

My wife felt the Holy Spirit say, "Just pray for her." She merely gave the woman a hug and quietly commanded the seizures to stop. Ever since that hug, the woman hasn't experienced another seizure. She was totally healed! Simple obedience releases the presence and power of God.

While Miranda is quick to pray or ask God to intervene, sometimes it takes me a little longer.

We were walking down the street in Vancouver about a year ago. As we passed by a homeless guy, the Lord said to me, "Go talk to him."

So I just walked up to him and said, "How are you doin'?"

And he said, "Good. I'm hungry."

"You're hungry?"

"Yeah. Can you buy me somethin' to eat?"

"Sure. Let's go." We started walking, and I asked, "Hey, man. Why are you here on the streets?"

"I hear voices in my head. I'm schizophrenic. It's been that way for years."

"After I buy you pizza, can I pray for you?"

The guy was so hungry for God, he said, "No. Not after the pizza. Now."

My wife and I laid hands on him. And immediately the fire of God went right through him. We cast the spirit out of him, and when we were done praying for him, we asked, "How do you feel now?"

"Dude. I can think for the first time in ten years. Clearly."

We fed him some pizza and preached the Gospel to him. He gave his life to the Lord.

I could tell you testimony, after testimony, after testimony because we're not just doing it from a pulpit. We're living it as a lifestyle. Just step out in obedience and you, too, will see miracles.

God wants to anoint you to do that. But first, He wants to go a little deeper into Philippians 2.

Humble Pie

You would think that talking about the miracles God does through you would put you in danger of becoming full of pride. It is a danger that I am well aware of. I've watched others stumble over their pride and fall. That is one fate that I want to be careful to avoid. Developing a continual awareness of humility seemed to be the key to avoiding pride. I definitely needed to know more. If we are going to carry the keys to the Kingdom with authority, and soar in the spirit, we need to know something about what humility truly is—and what it is not.

One time when I was with the Lord, I started asking Him about humility. "God, what does it mean to be humble?" I've heard a lot of preachers preaching on humility. And they always say, "Lower. Lower. We gotta go lower. Lower. Lower. Lower. Lower. Lower. We gotta go lower still."

Whenever I hear them, I wonder, "What is this? The limbo?" For those of you who don't know what the Limbo is, it's a childhood game where people try to go under a stick without falling off their feet. Who ever can go the lowest wins. "What does it mean to go lower in God? What is it to be humble?"

And the Lord spoke to me. "Jerame, to be truly humble in My sight is to do what I say when I say to do it. Anything outside of that is rebellion."

My heart sank. I hadn't thought of myself as rebellious.

"But, Jerame, it's OK." He said, "Jesus died on the cross. When you mess up, you can ask for forgiveness." And the Lord explained further, "True humility is to be obedient."

And I said, "Well show me that one in the Scriptures." God doesn't get mad if you challenge Him as friends. So I said, "Show me that one in the Scriptures."

He said, "Philippians chapter 2."

In verse five, I read the explanation I sought:

Let this mind be in you which also was in Christ Jesus, who being in the form of God, did not consider it robbery to be equal with God, but made Himself of no reputation, taking on the form of a bondservant and coming in the likeness of men. And being found in appearance as a man, He humbled Himself and became obedient [ding, ding, ding], to the point of death, even the death of the cross (Philippians 2:5-8).

Jesus humbled Himself and came in the likeness of men; He laid down His deity. He didn't grasp at it; He humbled Himself, and through obedience, He went to the cross and fulfilled the mandate that God had for Him. Do you want to know how you're going to fulfill the mandate that God has for you? Through obedience. Through intimacy with God and obedience to His voice. When you're obedient to His voice, it always manifests His glory.

We need to understand that Jesus did every miracle when He was on this earth *as a man*. He didn't do it as God *in His deity*.

Jesus made the way for everyone of us, and He did it as a man. There are no excuses to move into rebellion and say that temptation has overcome us, or decide not to act according to the word He gives us. Jesus was tempted and overcame it—as a man. The Bible says that He was tempted as we were tempted. The Bible also says that He overcame all temptations and as the great high priest fulfilled everything on our behalf (see Heb. 4:15). He knows what it feels like to be tempted; we know that when we fall short we can come to Him freely, without shame, and say, "Lord, forgive me."

You plead the blood. We can walk just like Jesus did on the earth if we begin to operate by spiritual principles and laws that are governed by His Word. Satan wanted to spoil it for us. But God continues to keep the way open to Himself.

Satan understood some things about Heaven. Why do you think the very temptation that he brought to Jesus was about turning stones into bread? Some think he chose that temptation because he wanted Jesus to fulfill His hunger. I don't think so. He tempted Jesus in that way because he was trying to get Him to grasp after His supernatural nature. Jesus gave us the key to walking in the miraculous and the supernatural when he adamantly rebuked satan: "The Lord rebuke you. Man shall not live on bread alone, but by every word that proceeds from the mouth of God" (see Matt. 4:4)

He was really saying, "satan, I will not grasp after My supernatural nature in Heaven because I must operate by the spiritual laws and principles that govern the Kingdom of God from the earth and see Heaven invade earth.

The Lord rebuke you. I'm not going to do this so that I can fulfill My own hunger because there is no manifest power outside of hearing God's voice. Satan, you know that the key to turning these stones into bread is hearing and obeying My Father's voice. I won't act on My own desires for salvation. I wait for Him. My Father will, and has, given Me the Kingdom. I trust His ways and timing—not yours."

Do you want to know what that anointing is? It's an anointing of sonship. It's an anointing of hearing God's voice and being obedient to what He says. And when you're obedient to what He says, awesome things happen.

God wants to give you an anointing of the counsel of God so that you can simply be obedient because when you're obedient, you're acting as a son, you're acting as a daughter.

The reason why we see so many miracles and salvations happen through us is because we keep the testimony of Jesus always before us. We talk about God stories. We anticipate that our friendship with Jesus will release greater encounters. And out of our intimate relationship, we just simply respond, "Lord, what do You want to do?" Then we say exactly what He says. We do exactly what He wants us to do. When we move in that realm of intimacy and obedience, the power of God shows up on a consistent basis.

God's going to raise up a whole generation who hear His voice, who know how to hear what He's saying. Out of a place of radical obedience, we are going to see some of the most amazing miracles and outpourings of the Holy Spirit that the world has ever seen.

Are you ready to step into radical relationship? Start talking about what you have seen and heard Him do. Expect more. Listen and step out in faithful obedience to what you hear Him saying. Get ready for more!

The Key

The key to opening portals of Heaven is in the power of the tongue. If you'll continue to develop an intimate relationship with Jesus—getting to the place where you can hear Him and then step out in obedience when you hear His voice—you will begin to see Him act on your behalf and through you on behalf of others. As you keep the testimony of what He is doing and has done foremost in your awareness, you'll have increasing encounters with God. God wants to give you encounters because He wants you to know His heart more and to release His heart to others. God wants to visit you, too, with angelic encounters, dreams, and visions.

Opening the Door

Lord, forgive me for not valuing the encounters You have given others and to me in the past. Help me to talk about them, to keep the testimony of Jesus alive when I talk to others, and to experience more of You. Give me an opportunity today to remember what You have done for me and speak it to another. Reveal more of Yourself to me. Come Holy Spirit!

CHAPTER 4

ASCENDING THE HIGH PLACES

Miranda and I were ministering at a church called Great Faith in Seoul, Korea; 3,000 to 4,000 hungry Koreans showed up every morning and every night, and God was also showing up to meet them in powerful ways. The first day of the meetings, ten deaf ears in a row opened up to total hearing. On the third or fourth day God prompted me to give a more specific altar call for people who had paralyzed right hands. I wondered how many people in the meeting could possibly fit that description, and to my surprise, seven people came forward. God healed five out of seven, on the spot, instantly. It seemed like we were ascending higher with God, drawing Heaven closer to earth as we ministered, experiencing creative miracles of a quantity and quality that we had not seen before. Something was different. And I asked the Lord what was going on.

During that trip, God visited me in a dream and gave me another key to unlock the future revolution of love.

In this dream, I was walking up this giant mountain, looking off into the distance as I hiked. The higher I got on the mountain, the clearer I could see in the valleys. Somehow I knew that it was the mountain of God.

After awhile, I looked toward the valley and saw a large tornado beginning to spin at a very high speed; everywhere it went it picked up trash and debris, and I could see it blowing around in the air. Yet it left something odd in its wake. Everywhere the tornado touched down, it left a golden brick road behind. It was so intriguing that I felt compelled to go higher so that I could see better. The adrenaline kicked in, and I practically ran up the mountain. To my surprise, a house sat near the top of the hill. So I went in the house and looked out the window. The storm was blowing closer, and I could see all the debris flying around, but I knew in my spirit it was a good storm. For some reason, I left the house and ran out the back door heading for the top of the hill. As often happens in dreams, right before I saw what happened next, I woke up.

Immediately upon waking, the Lord spoke to me and said, "Jerame, I want to send a powerful move of the Spirit to My people. I want to release a powerful move of the Spirit that will begin to affect entire regions. I want to release the winds of change in regions, in nations, and when I do this, it's going to take out all of the things that hinder the Church from the fullness of God—all the debris, all the trash, all that the enemy tries to toss in our way to hinder us. All the roadblocks are going to be removed, and there's going to be a clear path of the glory laid down for the people of God to walk on."

The Lord gave me another key. He said, "Ascending the hill of the Lord is the key to the Church coming into this powerful move in the Spirit, where the glory of God is revealed. I am calling people to make their home at the top of My holy mountain. I am looking for a Church that's a city on the hill that cannot be hidden, that will brightly shine for My glory."

Ever since I had the visitation, I've been consumed with studying the Word of God on the topic of mountains and have experienced further revelation through dreams and visions about this key dream. If we are going to see a powerful move in the Spirit in North America, we have to ascend the hill of the Lord as a Church.

Psalm 2 hints of this. Psalm 2 tells us that God wants us to begin to rule and reign from the high places. It talks about a scene where God is in the midst of a spiritual battle and all these people in the earth scoff at God, they mock Him and set themselves against God and against His anointed. In response, God from Heaven laughs at them. Then He offers us the nations as a gift—our inheritance.

> *Why do the nations rage, and the people plot a vain thing? The kings of the earth set themselves, and the rulers take counsel together, against the Lord and against His anointed, saying, "Let us break their bonds in pieces and cast away their cords from us." He who sits in the heavens shall laugh, the Lord shall hold them in derision. Then He shall speak to them in His wrath, and distress them in His deep displeasure. "Yet I have set My King on My holy hill of Zion." "I will decree the decree: the Lord has said to Me, 'You are My son, today I have begotten You. Ask of Me, and I will give You the nations for Your inheritance, and the ends of the earth for Your possession. You shall break them with a rod of iron; You shall dash them to pieces like a potter's vessel'"* (Psalm 2:1-9).

God is looking for a people who will ascend the hill of the Lord and be with their King. God desires intimacy, and the Bible says we're seated together in heavenly places (see Eph. 2:6). If Jesus' throne is on the mountain of God, then I want to go there. Why? Because I want to know Him more, and to see nations come to know Jesus Christ as Lord and as Savior. The dream that God gave me spoke to this—if the people of God will ascend the hill of the Lord, they will see a powerful move of the Spirit that will cause the glory of God to be revealed. Begin ascending the hill of the Lord and take your place with God in intimacy. Hear His voice and do what He says. When you do that, you can ask God for the inheritance of the nations, and He gives them to you and me and whosoever desires.

When we begin to live from a place of the mountaintops of God, encountering Him and His presence, we begin to rule and reign with a rod of iron. The devil's kingdom becomes fragile to the very words we speak, and we crush his kingdom as if it is just a bunch of pottery. We can speak at a meeting in a foreign country and crush the enemy as we release the power of God.

God is going to raise up a generation who will pray for the sick, and they will be instantly healed; when they prophesy things, they will come to pass. We're seeing God open up entire nations, giving authority to us to bring them into His glory. We are in a season where we are to ask God for the nations as our inheritance. God wants the Church to begin to think big. We need to think beyond the local church, our home group, or the four walls of our living rooms. God wants us to begin to believe that He can save a nation in a day. The Book of Isaiah says that God can birth an entire nation in one day (see Isa. 66:8).

I believe we are seeing God move powerfully through our ministry because we have been ascending the hill of the Lord, meeting Him on the summit, hearing God's voice, and doing what He says when He says to do it. Then, in places like Korea, and even in the United States, breakthrough happens. Intimacy with God and obedience to His voice cause the manifestation of His glory.

When I went to Seoul, Korea, for the very first time a couple of years ago, those who invited me said they hadn't experienced much healing or other manifestations of God's power. Their building seated about 2,000 people at that time. During the first night of the conference, the Lord said, "Jerame, I want you to release the rod of God. I don't want you to preach. These people need to see power. Demonstrate My power."

So I opened with ministry, and 13 deaf ears were healed as the power of God came into the meeting. A woman who had been crippled for years was brought in on a mat, completely paralyzed. As we released a healing wave of power, all we could hear was *crack, crack, crack,* and she jumped up and was instantly healed. We simply released the power of God for another two days, then went home to the United States.

Three months later, I went back to the church, and in this short amount of time, they'd moved into a building that holds 4,000 to 5,000 people. Their church membership skyrocketed from 16,000 to 32,000. The leaders attributed the move of God's power to the amazing growth. One of the leaders said, "Jerame, since the day you and Miranda came, imparted to us, and released the rod of God, every single pastor and associate pastor has moved in the same miracles you saw. We have not had a worship service without the glory of God breaking out in signs and wonders since you left."

That's the power of impartation and ruling and reigning in the nations with the rod of iron to crush the strongholds of the enemy.

God wants to do something big in every city—and not just cities, but whole nations at a time.

It is all about the high places. Every king in the Old Testament was judged by this—whether they ripped down the Ashtoreth poles of rebellious worship to false gods and established worship to the Lord in the high places. God wants you to bring down strongholds in your city and region, in your state and even your country.

How do we begin to ascend the mountain? When we praise God, giving Him all of our hearts, there is something established of the mountain of God in our spirits.

From the high places of worship, we can dethrone things that have hindered the fullness of the Kingdom that we are coming into. But I want you to understand something. It is going to take more than just one person fully giving of himself or herself to worship and ascending the mountain of the Lord through high praises. It is going to take more than just a couple of people holding microphones, who are anointed and have itinerant ministries. This is about the Body of Christ awakening to their inheritance, knowing who they are in Christ.

Our inheritance is the nations. We ascend the mountain of the Lord through worship, but once we get to the top, what do we see? The house in my dream is the throne of God. The reason why God wants us to ascend the mountain of God is because His throne resides on top of the mountain (see Ps. 2:6). Once we get there, we see that we are seated with Him in heavenly places, and we take up our authority to rule and reign with Him. But there is a condition. You have to lighten up. You have to drop any impure thing you've been carrying around.

Psalm 24 asks,

Who may ascend the hill of the Lord? Or who may stand in His holy place? He who has clean hands and a pure heart, who has not lifted up his soul to an idol, nor sworn deceitfully (Psalm 24:3-4).

God wants you to come before Him in the holy place and encounter Him, but don't worry: He will not toss you out. He is a God of grace. The Book of Hebrews says that God has granted us boldness to come before His throne of grace in our time of need to receive what He has for us—forgiveness (see Heb. 4:16). He urges us to come boldly before the throne of grace.

We are going to ascend the hill of the Lord through clean hands and a pure heart, through not lifting up our souls to an idol. I don't care what kind of sin you are in; Jesus paid the price on the cross. His hands were pierced, and He was pierced for our transgression, for our sins. So God's taken care of the sin part. If you have sin in your life, if you have dirty hands, you can't stand in the holy place. God won't allow you to because it will kill you. He's a Holy God. What you could get away with in some places will kill you when you start to climb higher up the mountain and closer to His glory.

If you understand Jesus and His sacrifice—that He gave it all for us, that while we were yet sinners, He loved us, and the blood purchased everything we need to overcome sin, that He was raised from the dead—you can ascend the hill of God.

He took care of the hands, but you have to take care of the heart.

It's your decision to what extent you are going to live for God. Are you going to live halfway committed, or are you going to live fully committed?

We are going to see some of the most powerful men and women of God who have ever walked the face of the earth, and it's not going to be just because they are gifted; it's going to be because they have a radical intimacy with God. It's going to be because they have clean hands and a pure heart. When I say a pure heart, I mean that they have decided that they are going to live fully for God.

This is a time and a season of demarcation; this is a time and a season when God is making a distinction between those who love Him and those who don't (see Mal. 3:18). God is looking for a generation of no compromise and purity.

I believe that God wants to rewrite the understanding of what it is to have a lifestyle of no compromise and purity. In the past, the Church taught us that purity is a list of don'ts—don't do this, and don't do that. But that's called legalism, and legalism causes more sin to occur. Put rules on people, and they want to break them. God sent the Holy Spirit, not a preacher, to convict men and women of their sin. God didn't send your mother to convict you of sin. It's a relationship thing. If you have a relationship with God, and you develop the ability to know and to hear Him, you will not do the things that displease Him.

God is looking for a sold-out generation who will walk in power. He's raising up an army, and, according to the Word, in the day of His power, His troops will willingly volunteer. This generation will be marked by their burning passion for Jesus. They're going to be the ones who care about nothing else but Jesus and Jesus alone, and long to see His Kingdom invade every facet of life on this earth. They are going to do it by ascending the hill of God.

If we're that much in love with the Lord and led by the Spirit of God, we won't fall into the traps of the enemy. This is what true purity is: no compromise because we are so in love and focused on Jesus.

Here is a simple test to see how close you are to hearing the voice of the Holy Spirit and how open you are to pleasing the Lord. Next time you're watching something on television or are tempted with something that usually doesn't affect you, just say, "Holy Spirit, does this please You?"

If you feel a weight or sadness, as if He grieves in you, and you sense that it would be better for you to turn off the television show or turn away from what has been a "normal" activity for you, then listen to that inner prompting. It may not seem like sin, but it is likely separating you from the Lord. God wants us to take a step further into the Kingdom and say, "I want more of You, God, and I'm willing to sacrifice good things to get the best."

God wants us to have no idols before Him. God wants us to put Him before everything in our lives— before our family, our careers, our ministries. God wants to be number one in our lives and to fellowship with us on a higher level.

Climb a little higher, and you will stand in the holy place before God.

Promotion will happen. A greater release of authority happens when you stand on that hill with Him.

God is releasing a violent spirit of faith from Heaven to seek His face like Jacob. Remember the story of Jacob who wrestled with an angel all night long until the angel touched him and broke his hip? Suddenly, he walked with a limp and entered into a new name and a new identity. We pay a price when we sell out for God. I'm telling you, what He wants to give us will far outweigh the pleasures of this world.

The mountain of God is an alone place. Like Jacob, you will have a secret place where you wrestle with angels and the supernatural. It's the place of encounter. It's a place of intimacy with God. Jesus would often leave His followers and the things of this world to ascend the mountain to pray. If He needed to be alone with His Father, how much more do we need to turn off the television and the video games and ascend the mountain to be with Him?

I'm reminded of the story when Jesus fed the five thousand. He took them on the mountain and gave thanks there. As He began to pass out bread, it multiplied. The miracle happened from the mountaintop. Jesus had a lifestyle of getting alone with His Father, and because of that, He always saw amazing words and miracles released through Him. Right after Jesus multiplied the bread, He sent His disciples to the other side of the Galilee and said He would meet them there.

He sent the disciples away, sent the people they fed away, and He went to the mountain by Himself with God. Instead of waiting until the disciples rowed halfway across the Sea of Galilee, He decided to walk to them on the water. He walked from the mountaintop onto the sea. Intimacy with God equals stepping into the supernatural. He walked up to the boat and freaked everybody out; they thought He was a ghost. But Peter said, "Lord, if it's really You, tell me to come." God wants us to ask Him things. God wants us to place a demand on the friendship we have with Him.

He wants us to say, "Lord, how do I do this? How do I walk? How do I live in the supernatural? How do I live in Your power?" Peter discovered a principle that God wants to give us. Do you want to know why he was able to walk on the water? Because he asked. And because God spoke it to him first, and said come.

Intimacy with God and obedience to His voice causes the manifestation of the supernatural. If you'll begin to live a lifestyle of ascending the hill of the Lord, a lifestyle of praying and intimacy with God, it will change who you are, and you will begin to walk in the supernatural.

We keep moving from one supernatural event to another. Right after Jesus and Peter got back in the boat, the Bible says that ***immediately*** they were on the other side: they were transported. They didn't have to row across the rest of that extremely wide lake—a lake so wide it is called a sea. I mean, isn't this fun! This is Jesus, the man of miracles, inviting us into greater things than we can imagine.

Transportation in the Glory

Speaking of transportations, in the last chapter, I told a testimony about how God transported my brother Josh, my friend Craig, and me from Vancouver, Canada, to Mississippi. We have experienced this phenomena several times. I remember another time we got transported while in Guayaquil, Ecuador. I was down there with a good friend of mine for a two-week ministry trip to both Peru and Ecuador with a team of about 70 youth. While we were there, we did nightly crusades and daily outreaches in the streets; we ministered to the orphans and even fed the poor. It was a blast.

For two weeks we did nothing but preach the Gospel and spend time loving on the poor. On that trip we saw an amazing harvest of souls. Over 5,000 people gave their lives to the Lord, and we saw many notable, remarkable miracles—tumors dissolving, blind eyes seeing, deaf ears hearing, and even cripples walking! Then, as the trip came to an end, we all went to Guayaquil, Ecuador, to catch our flights back home to the United States.

On our last day in Ecuador, a group of us decided to go shopping. We ended up walking with our tour guide about two hours away from our hotel to find some good places to buy some clothes. While walking along, I began to miss spending time with God alone. You see, we spent all of our week just pouring out our time and energy toward preaching and loving people. We didn't really have any time at all to spend with Jesus that week. So as my friends went into the stores to shop, I began to become desperate for more of God.

I said to God, "Lord, I need to be filled back up with Your presence. All I have done for the past few weeks is pour out Your love. I need a touch of Your glory. Holy Spirit, come, fill me up!"

I began to remember the promise that Jesus gave to the people of His day in John 7:37-39. On the last day of the great feast, He told them, *"If anyone thirsts, let him come to Me and drink. He who believes in Me, as the Scripture has said, out of his heart will flow rivers of living water"* (John 7:37-38). He was speaking of the Holy Ghost. So right there on a street corner in Ecuador, I told the Lord, "God, I am so hungry; I'm so thirsty for more of You, Lord. I want to drink freely of Your river of life."

By faith, I began to drink of the Holy Ghost. With my hands, I made imaginary shot glasses, and I started taking shots of living water right there in front of everyone on the street corner. I must have taken at least two hundred shots of living water by faith. Suddenly it was like pure joy entered into my soul, and I began to laugh out loud, uncontrollably. It was awesome, and it was exactly what I needed. I began to be filled with joy unspeakable and full of glory. It was like God was filling me back up and recharging my spirit just as you would recharge your cell phone. I was physically exhausted yet felt the strength of God coming into me.

Then my friends came out of the store and watched me. They were kind of embarrassed of me and said, "What are you doing? Why are you acting so crazy?"

I said, "I don't care what you guys think about me. It's been two weeks since I have had any time with Jesus, and I want Him now!"

Then I just started drinking more, and more, and more. All of a sudden it was like I won my friends over, and they started drinking of the river of life by faith as well. We began to laugh out loud and speak in tongues and enjoy God, giving Him praise right there on the street corner.

Eventually, one of my friends said to me, "I'm hungry for food."

So we asked our tour guide to take us somewhere to eat, and he told us that we had to walk all the way back to the hotel because there was nothing worth eating in that part of the city. So we just kept enjoying God's presence, walked for about a block, and turned the corner.

Then our tour guide suddenly started freaking out, pointing his finger up at this sign, and screaming, "We're here! We're here! How did this happen?"

Right there in front of our eyes, we saw our hotel and a sign in front of us that said, "Dinner Special, Chicken $5.95."

Our tour guide was freaking out because we had walked over two hours away from the hotel, and God, in an instant of time, transported us from one physical location to another. God does amazing things when you hunger and thirst after Him. We were all shocked and excited at the same time and went into the hotel and ate dinner.

Later the Lord began to teach me different keys to stepping into these kinds of encounters.

The first thing He told me was this: "Jerame, you entered into this experience because you were hungering and thirsting to encounter Me, and you didn't care what anybody thought. You simply wanted Me."

The Key of Hunger

Supernatural things will happen when you want to know God more. The Bible says in Matthew 5:6, *"Blessed are those who hunger and thirst for righteousness, for they shall be filled."*

As you seek to know God more, as you desire to ascend the mountain of God and stand with Him in His holy place, God responds to your hunger and begins to pour out His Spirit upon you. Acts 2:17-19 says that God will pour out His spirit on all flesh, that the sons and daughters of God shall prophesy, and that people will have dreams and visions and see God move in signs, wonders, and miracles. When God pours out His Spirit on you, you will have supernatural encounters with Him.

I believe that God is restoring to us as a Church the ability to walk in the supernatural like the early church did. One of the greatest keys to entering into this aspect of the Kingdom is hunger. You see, when God can find a genuine hunger, He can pour out His Spirit. The other key is to lose your dignity. So many people are so afraid of what people think. God wants to set us free from the fear of man and make us as bold as a lion. God is raising up a generation who will not be afraid to worship their King in public. They will be a generation of lovesick worshipers who become signs and wonders for God (see Isa. 8:18). They will become like Daniel who worshiped and prayed to God—not in a place of hiding, but right in front of his window, three times a day for all to see—even when it was illegal to pray to or worship any other god than Darius, the king of Babylon. Intimacy will be more important to them than what people think of them.

The second thing that God said to me was this: "Tell My people that if they will have a heart to preach My Gospel, they will experience supernatural things. When you do Kingdom things, Kingdom things happen."

I asked Him, "What do you mean, when you do Kingdom things, Kingdom things happen?"

He said, "Jerame, what have you been doing all week? It was because you were preaching the Kingdom that you received the Kingdom."

Afterward, I began to think about this, and I realized what He was saying. We had been doing crusades, feeding the poor, and loving people nobody cared about. We were preaching a Gospel of Heaven invading earth.

You see, what you preach is what you get. If you are preaching a message of repentance, you will get repentance, and if you are preaching a message of healing, you will get healing. So if you are preaching a message like Jesus preached—of Heaven invading earth—then Heaven will begin to invade the earth wherever that message is preached.

You get what you preach and what you have faith for.

It was as Jesus went out preaching the Gospel of the Kingdom of God that His Father would work with Him and confirm His word with supernatural signs and wonders following. Later on, after Jesus ascended into Heaven, God also worked with His disciples. Mark 16:20 says, *"And they* [the disciples] *went out and preached everywhere, the Lord working with them and confirming the word through the accompanying signs."*

As I began to look at the Bible, I saw that in many places there was a connection between preaching the Gospel and the supernatural. In the Book of Acts 8:26-39, Philip has two supernatural encounters that were triggered by preaching the Gospel. First of all, in Acts 8:12-13, right after Philip preaches the Gospel in Samaria, revival breaks out in the city. The Lord sends an angel to him and tells him to go south along the road, which goes down from Jerusalem to Gaza. As Philip went in obedience to the word of the Lord, he ran into an Ethiopian eunuch, a man of great authority in charge of the Queen of Ethiopia's treasury. When Philip met the man, he was reading the Book of Isaiah and asked Philip to interpret it. Then Philip preached the Gospel to the eunuch, and the man decided to give his life to Jesus and be baptized on the spot.

When Philip put him under the water and brought him up out of the water, the Spirit of the Lord came and swept Philip away to another place, leaving the eunuch by himself in the water (see Acts 8:39). You see, it was as Philip was preaching the Gospel to the eunuch that the supernatural began to take place. God always confirms His Word with signs and wonders. It was because we were preaching the Gospel that we began to experience the supernatural everywhere we were going. That is another reason why we got transported.

A Kingdom momentum begins to take place when you do Kingdom things. The more you step out and be like Jesus, the more God releases to you. For instance, if you want a powerful healing anointing, then step out and pray for the sick. You can be 100 percent sure that you won't experience seeing the sick healed if you don't ever step out sometime and do it. God is looking for a generation who will step out in faith and preach the Gospel of the Kingdom message that Jesus preached and expect that Heaven will back them up. You get what you preach. If you believe and have faith for the supernatural, it will begin to happen. God wants you to believe for His Kingdom to invade every part of your life.

If you are hungry, you are bound to seek for an abundance—not just scrounge for a little. God wants us to have more!

The Key

The key to moving in signs and wonders is to hunger after Jesus and His Kngdom. As you seek to know God more, as you desire to ascend the mountain of God and stand with Him in His holy place, God responds to your hunger and begins to pour out His spirit upon you. Acts 2:17-19 says that God will pour out His spirit on all flesh, that the sons and daughters of God shall prophesy, and that people will have dreams and visions and see God move in signs, wonders, and miracles. When God pours out His Spirit on you, you will have supernatural encounters with Him.

Opening the Door

Lord, I am hungry for more of You. Please come and release the abundance of Your anointing to me and through me so that others who hunger for You may see You and believe in You when I step out and give away all that You have given me. Increase my heart to speak about who You are and how amazing, alive, and powerful You are. Back me up with signs and wonders that testify to Your presence and power to seek and save the lost. Here am I, send me!

CHAPTER 5

KEYS TO THE ABUNDANCE OF THE ANOINTING

There comes a time in everyone's relationship with God when we know we are so human that it would take a miracle to make us look, act, and move in power like Jesus. We need to be transfigured in His glory to see His glory, and to release His glory to others. In the Bible, only three disciples experienced Jesus' transfiguration. Jesus' transfiguration on the mountain became their own, deeply personal encounter, which likely strengthened them to do great exploits and run the race of their destinies.

One thing that encounter did for sure was enable the disciples to see Jesus in a different light. And as they saw Him in a different light, they saw themselves differently. They became more open to Heaven interacting with earth, and the cloud of witnesses became real rather than words written on a page or passed down in spoken legends. They began to realize that the anointing on Jesus' life was theirs as well, on earth. He passed along the key to the abundance of the anointing through revelatory encounters. The key that Jesus released to me that unlocked the abundance of the anointing in my life was not a real key. In fact, it was more like a formula. But we'll get to that revelatory encounter in just another page or two. In the meantime, let's take a look at the transfiguration.

In Luke 9, Jesus took Peter, James, and John with Him and ascended a mountain in order to spend time praying. In that time of prayer, the appearance of His face and His body was transfigured and consumed in heavenly glory. Peter, James, and John are watching this from a little distance away on the mountain. And as they're watching Jesus pray, Elijah and Moses appear and start talking to Jesus. Jesus is having a cloud-of-witnesses experience. He knew that the two men talking to Him were the Old Testament patriarchs Elijah and Moses who had gone on to Heaven long before Jesus left for earth and who are part of the great cloud of witnesses talked about in Hebrews 12:1-2. That great cloud of witnesses in Heaven cheer us on as they look down into our time. It is as if they're up there looking to see what God's going to do here. They're up there yelling, "Go, Church, Go! Go, Church, Go!"

Elijah and Moses talked to Jesus about His death and resurrection, about when He was going to be raised from the dead, and of the future glory to be revealed. They came after Jesus had already ascended the mountain many times to be alone with His Father, listening. They came at the call of the Father to go to His Son—before His hour of need. Encounters in the supernatural are released to us to bring revelation regarding God's Kingdom and His plans. Spiritual encounters are given by God so that we would know Him more. Jesus was in constant contact with the Father, but He needed something more to strengthen Him for the tormenting death He was about to face. He needed to be transfigured and taste a glimpse of His Kingdom. If Jesus needed that encounter, how much more do we?

God wants us to ascend the hill of the Lord and, along the way, to encounter God in His glory and become transfigured into something more Christ-like. We are changed as He causes us to come into a greater revelation of who He is and who we are. When Peter and James and John were on the mountain and saw Jesus transfigured in glory right in front of their eyes, Peter said something kind of stupid, "Lord, it's good for us to be here. How about we make three tabernacles, one for You, one for Elijah, one for Moses?" (see Luke 9:33).

Suddenly, a glory cloud came down out of Heaven, overshadowed Peter, James, and John, and scared them to death as a voice from Heaven spoke, urging them to listen to Him. "He is My Son in who I am well pleased."

Jesus got transfigured, but the disciples also entered into their own encounter with the Father that led them to see Jesus differently—not so familiarly. Suddenly Jesus wasn't just a guy they hung out with. Jesus became more understandably the Son of God.

You see, that day Peter was getting a revelation that Jesus was different than Moses and Elijah—that Jesus was the Son of God. Your encounters with God should also enable you to understand Jesus in a greater light. God wants to give you encounters so you will know who Christ is and so you will begin to walk in the things of God. You can't walk as a son and a daughter of God until you know Christ and until you know who you are in Christ.

Be bold. Go and encounter Jesus on the mountain.

The whole purpose of encountering the transfiguration—or the glory of God—is to give you a greater revelation of the Father's love and a greater revelation of who Jesus is. This will result in us coming into a greater revelation of His Kingdom, and a greater revelation of His authority and His power.

When you begin to have encounters with God in the glory, His power will also be released.

In fact, right after the mount of transfiguration, Luke 9:37-42 says that Peter, James, John, and Jesus came off the mountain and saw a crowd of people waiting for Him. Jesus came up to this crowd and heard that some of His disciples had been trying to cast a demon out of a child, but they couldn't do it. Jesus just walked over to the scene, told them they are full of unbelief and simply said, "Come out!" And the child was healed.

Jesus walked around in great authority, healing and delivering people. In fact, He had more authority than any other person in His time, and the Bible says that He would cast demons out with a word. Why could He do that when no one else could? Because He was being filled up on the top of the mountain with His God, and He was having encounters with the Holy Spirit where He began to shine in the glory. He carried the authority of Heaven that He obtained on the mountaintop back down into the earth and manifested it. We can, too. In fact, He is releasing His authority to you and to me to do even greater works than the ones Jesus did in the Bible. You need to spend time with Him—and then step out in faith.

One time I was in Hudson's Hope, British Colum-bia, where I was scheduled to be part of three days of revival meetings. During the first night of the meetings, I had the night off from speaking but went to support the other speakers and listen to what they had to share. The worship was awesome, and there was such a sweet presence of God in the room. I remember being so hungry for Jesus, all I wanted to do was worship Him. After the meeting ended, the conference hosts took me back to the home I was staying at and fed me, and I decided to turn in early as I was scheduled to preach first thing in the morning. Walking to my room, I thought about how good the worship was and how much I wanted to just be in the presence of God. I decided to put on my iPod and worship the Lord for a few minutes as I drifted off to sleep. So I closed my eyes, listened to my iPod, and began to tell God how hungry I was to know Him more. After about two minutes of just softly praising the Lord, I felt the sweetest presence of God come into my room. Then it intensified. I opened my eyes, and much to my surprise, in the natural I could see what seemed to be a real glory cloud in my room.

It surrounded my bed, and I could feel God so strongly; it was like I was buzzing in the glory. This experience lasted for about five minutes, and then it faded away. This was the first time I had ever seen a glory cloud. In a state of great peace, I fell asleep and woke up the next day to get ready for the meetings.

That morning as I began to minister the Lord showed up in great power. A man who had hurt his back lifting a snowmobile was instantly healed as we prayed for him; another with arthritis was healed; and deafness left people's ears. Then bizarre miracles began to happen without anyone laying hands upon individuals. One little girl came up to me and asked, "Can God heal me too? I need my teeth to be healed." She smiled and showed me her really crooked teeth. Then I just said to her, "In the name of Jesus, be healed." I just spoke the word. I didn't even lay hands on her. She left, and I continued praying for others. A few minutes later she came up to me to show me that her teeth had been completely straightened out. It was awesome!

During the night session as I was preaching, the Lord told me that He was going to begin to sovereignly deliver people in His glory. He told me to stop preaching and release His presence. So I did exactly what He said.

I stopped preaching and prayed that God would release His glory into the room. When I did this, a woman on the left side of the platform fell on the ground and began screaming at the top of her lungs. Immediately the pastors ran over to her to see what was wrong with her and take control over the situation. As they did this, the Lord told me to tell them to stop and let the Lord have His way with her. So I told them what God had just said to me about her while the women kept screaming for a few more minutes. Suddenly, this amazing peace descended on her, and she was totally calm. I asked her what had happened. She then began to tell me that her whole life she had been attacked by demonic spirits of fear and anxiety. She had been to many deliverance specialists and had many powerful ministers pray for her, and no one could help her. Then, as we prayed and asked God to release His glory, she fell into a trance-like experience, and the Lord gave her revelation as to why she was always attacked and could not stop it.

In the vision she saw her grandmother hold her up to the sky and dedicate her life to satan. When her grandmother did this, she saw chains begin to bind her. As the vision continued, Jesus appeared with a sword and cut the chains off of her! She was instantly set free after this experience in the natural. Later, she testified to the people that she was fully set free from the fear and anxiety, and the attacks of the enemy for the first time in her whole life. You see, it was just like the passage we talked about earlier where Jesus' disciples could not cast a devil out of the little boy, but Jesus could because He had just been on the mountain with His Father.

I had just had my own encounter with God's glory cloud, and the results of that encounter were that miracles, signs, and wonders happened, and even this woman was set free from the demonic. We need to begin to ascend the mountain of God until we come into contact with the manifest presence of God. Then, when we come down off the mountain or out of our prayer time with God, we begin to carry the substance of the authority of Heaven into the natural realm of this earth to set others free from demonic strongholds, sickness, and disease. Authority is released when you encounter the glory of God.

If Jesus needed encounters with the counsel of Heaven to do what He did on the earth, we do too. Sometimes, Jesus talked directly to the Father. In this case, Moses and Elijah visited Him. I want you to understand something; God will visit us any way He wants to: He'll visit us in a cloud of glory, through dreams, visions, an angel, or even by sending us one or two from the great cloud of witnesses.

I have had a cloud-of-witnesses experience. Every time you have an encounter with something like this, it's to release revelation of God's heart for us, to speak of things that affect His Kingdom, or to give direction for where we should go. It may also release to you a greater anointing in order to affect the Kingdom.

One day I was spending time with God, speaking in tongues, and all of a sudden, I went into a vision. Before me appeared Isaiah the prophet.

We were sitting in front of a stone table that had Isaiah 55:1-3 etched into it. Suddenly this crazy prophet slams down a cup that looks like a goblet. Then he places a bottle of wine next to it and adds a jar of honey and some milk. He takes some from each, pours it into the goblet and mixes it up. Then he hands it to me.

I take it, and I drink the liquid of "joy unspeakable, full of glory." I mean, I was filled with the joy of the Lord. After I came out of the encounter, I immediately asked God what that was all about.

He said, "Jerame, I just gave you the formula for the abundance of the anointing of God. Read the verses that were on the stone table."

I went to Isaiah 55 and was amazed by what it said:

*Ho! Everyone who thirsts, come to the waters; and you who have no money, come, buy and eat. Yes, come, buy wine and milk without money and without price. Why do you spend money for what is not bread, and wages for what does not satisfy? Listen carefully to Me, and eat what is good, and let your **soul delight itself in abundance**. Incline your ear, and come to Me. Hear, and your soul shall live; and I will make an everlasting covenant with you—the sure mercies of David* (Isaiah 55:1-3).

Anytime I have a supernatural encounter, I say, "Lord where's that at in the Word? Show it to me." Because if God can't show it to me in the Word, I don't think it's from Him. If the experiences that we have with God don't line up with what His Word says, we shouldn't accept them. God's not blessing flaky Christianity. God is after a people who know their God. Those who know God and His Word will do mighty exploits for His Kingdom (see Dan. 11:32). God made it easy on me in this encounter. This vision came with the Word etched in stone.

You see, the Lord sent Isaiah the prophet to me in the vision for the purpose of bringing further revelation to the very words that he wrote so that, as a Church, we can begin to access the anointing of Heaven. Do you want an abundant anointing? The Amplified translation states that this is an anointing of fatness. Do you want a fat anointing on your life? In this encounter, God gave me the ingredients.

He said, "Jerame, the ingredients to an anointing of fatness are the honey, the milk, and the wine. The milk is the milk of the Word, the wine is the wine of My presence, and the honey is prophetic revelation."

The Keys to an Abundant Anointing

After this encounter, I began to search out what God told me, and found out that everything He told me about lined up with His Word. In the Word, I first took a look at the ingredients the Lord gave me for an abundant anointing—the ingredients of the milk, wine, and honey.

First, let's look at the "milk of the Word." After the Lord told me that the milk of the Word was one of the keys to stepping into an abundant anointing, I knew He was talking about the Scripture found in First Peter 2:2. It reads, *"As newborn babes, desire the pure milk of the word, that you may grow thereby."*

The people of God need to have the Word of God in their lives—it's the very nutrition that they live by. They need to begin to partake of the milk of the Word until they possess a strong foundation of the Word and become mature. Just as a baby in the natural needs milk to grow so it can become strong, healthy, and mature, so do the people of God need to begin to drink the milk of the Word so that they can become strong, healthy, and mature. You see, if you are faithful with little, God will give you much. There are too many people out there who are trying to just eat the meat of God's Word. They want all the deep things of God but are unwilling to pay the price necessary to obtain them by diving into the Word of God. We need to become students of the Word. If you will drink the milk of the Word and be faithful to strengthen your foundation in the Word, then God will entrust you with more. That "more" is the meat of the Word found in Hebrews 5:14: *"But solid food belongs to those who are of full age, that is, those who by reason of use have their senses exercised to discern both good and evil."*

Now let's talk about the new wine of Heaven. The new wine is the presence of God. Paul talked about the presence of God being like wine in Ephesians 5:18. He said, "Do not be drunk with wine in the natural, but be filled with the Spirit of God." Why would Paul compare being filled with the Holy Spirit to drinking wine? What was he saying? I believe God wants us to come under the influence of the Holy Spirit. Just as someone who gets drunk in the natural begins to do and say things he or she would not normally do, so God wants us to partake of His presence until we come under the influence of the Holy Spirit and begin to say and do things that we would not normally do in our natural abilities.

God is looking for a generation who will value His presence above all things in this world. He is looking for a people who will drink in the new wine of His presence and step into the supernatural nature of His Spirit. I believe that one of the keys to walking in God's power and the supernatural life is spending time with God drinking in His presence. In the last chapter, I told the testimony of how God transported us from one physical location to another in no time in Ecuador. What caused us to step into this experience was my hunger to drink in God's love. In that story, I drank hundreds of shot glasses full of the presence of God by faith.

After that experience, the Lord told me, "Jerame, the reason why you stepped into that encounter was because you were hungering and thirsting for My presence."

Then later He told me this, "Tell my people this: if they will begin to drink of wine of My presence, they will begin to be influenced by My Spirit and step into the deep things of the Spirit."

The end result of drinking in the new wine of Heaven in Ecuador was stepping into the supernatural realms of God. It was because we were intoxicated with the new wine of Heaven, or under the influence of the Holy Spirit, that we stepped out of the natural realm and into the supernatural realm.

Now let's take a look at the honey. After reading Isaiah 55:1-3, I saw the milk and the wine clearly revealed, but didn't see the honey. So I asked the Lord, "Show me how the honey fits into this equation. Where does the Word show honey as prophetic revelation? Where is that in the Word?"

Immediately, the Lord answered, "I promised my people that they would enter into a land of abundance that is overflowing with milk and honey (see Exod. 3:8). You see, the milk and the honey go hand in hand. The milk is the Word of God, and the honey is the anointing of prophetic revelation."

After the Lord spoke this to me, the Holy Spirit began to show me several examples of the Word and prophetic revelation or honey working together. The first example was found in the Book of Ezekiel chapter 3:1-3. It says,

> *Moreover He said to me, "Son of man, eat what you find; eat this scroll, and go, speak to the house of Israel." So I opened my mouth, and He caused me to eat that scroll. And He said to me, "Son of man, feed your belly, and fill your stomach with this scroll that I give you." So I ate, and it was in my mouth like honey in sweetness.*

This passage clearly shows the connection between the Word of God (the milk) and the anointing of prophetic revelation (the honey).

In this story, God fed Ezekiel a scroll. The end result of Ezekiel eating this scroll was that it tasted like honey in his mouth. He was then commanded to go and speak the Word of the Lord to all of Israel. You see, when God begins to fill you with His Word, it will become revelation in your mouth, and you will have the ability to speak His inspired Word to others.

John also had a similar encounter to the one Ezekiel experienced in the Book of Revelation 10:9-11. In this Scripture, an angel handed John a book and told him to eat it. Then, as John ate that book, it became sweet like honey in his mouth but bitter in his stomach. He was then commanded to prophesy to people, nations, and kings. This is the second time in Scripture that you see honey and the Word go together. The Word and the Spirit go hand in hand to bring revelation to the individual, and then through him or her to others. Notice in this Scripture it says that it was sweet like honey in his mouth and bitter in his stomach. Sometimes as God shows us things about people, places, or nations through revelation, we can see things in the Spirit that are scary or cause the giver of the word to be bitter toward giving the word. The result is that it is not always easy to give a word of correction or judgement. For example, I have a spiritual father who is a seer prophet. He was in Singapore and had a vision of the hand of God throwing down a principality out of the sky. In his vision he saw a half lion, half fish creature being thrown out of the heavens, and when it hit the earth it smashed into the ocean. Then a huge earthquake came causing huge tsunami waves to happen. After the prophet saw this in the vision the Lord commanded him to prophesy that God was removing an ancient principality from the southeast Asia region that held back revival in Southeast Asia. The Lord told him to publicly prophesy what he saw in a large revival meeting he was doing while in Singapore, and that what he saw would happen after he left the country. Then one day later he got on a plane to leave Singapore to go back home to Canada, and a few hours after his plane left the earthquake of December 2004 hit which caused massive destruction and a huge tsunami wave to occur. At the time of the vision the prophet said he did not want to give the word but the Lord kept telling him to prophesy what he saw. This is an example of the things of revelation being sweet but yet bitter. Since that time until now over 100,000 souls have come into the kingdom in Southeast Asia!

Another example of honey symbolizing an anointing of prophetic revelation is in First Samuel 14:24-30. In this passage, Saul called upon the people of God to fast during a time that was supposed to release great victory over the enemy. Saul declared that no one in the kingdom was allowed to eat anything before evening. As Saul did this, the people, as well as the army of Israel, walked through a forest over ground that was covered with honey. Jonathon followed behind the camp of Israel; he had not heard the decree given by his father. So he took his rod, dipped it in the honey, tasted it, and his eyes were enlightened (see 1 Sam. 14:27). When you begin to partake of the honey of God, it will bring enlightenment—your eyes will be open to see.

God wants us to begin to partake of the milk, the wine, and the honey every day. When we have the milk of the Word and the wine of His presence, and combine it with the honey—which is the prophetic revelation anointing—it produces the anointing of abundance or fatness in our lives.

That's an abundant anointing.

Over the years, I have been ardently pursuing the wine of His presence and diving deep into the Word. In the process, I've felt my heart enlarge and long for His glory to be released to the world in a greater way than the world has ever known. The key, or formula, for the anointing was mixing in me. Eventually, it came out in an abundant anointing—a big, fat anointing that releases the power and presence of God to a lost and hungry world.

In Indonesia, we were in a stadium with 6,000 Muslims, and, as I mentioned in the first chapter, on the opening night of the meeting, five deaf ears in a row opened on the platform because God told me to call the deaf forward for healing. When I came to pray for the last one, a little girl about seven years old who had never heard a sound out of her right ear because she didn't even have an ear hole, just a flap of skin, God did a creative miracle. He gave her a brand-new ear.

Before that meeting, I ascended that mountain of God, prayed with Jesus, and sought His face about what He wanted me to do. When you connect with God, you ascend the hill and gain His strategy. If you want to be a voice, you've got to speak from the mountaintops. Whatever He speaks to you on the mountaintop, shout from the rooftops...or whatever platform God gives you (see Matt. 10:27).

That miracle shattered the meeting and opened up 6,000 people to encounter the real God—Jesus Christ. That night thousands of Muslims got saved, and many hardened street kids ran forward and gave their lives to the Lord. As a result, we got invited to the governor's house, preached the Gospel there, and watched God move in signs and wonders and confirm things in the heavens. The next night we were live on television to 2 million Muslims who were longing to see the glory of God.

In Seoul, Korea, as I mentioned in Chapter 4, I opened with ministry, and five people with paralyzed right hands were healed; later, thirteen deaf ears were healed as the power of God came into another meeting. A woman who had been crippled for years was brought in on a mat, completely paralyzed. As we released a healing wave of power, all we could hear was *crack, crack, crack,* and she jumped up and was instantly healed.

The wine of Jesus' presence was released to them and healed them. The milk of His Word made them realize that healing is the children's bread and available to them always. And the honey of prophetic revelation released the strategy that enabled them to drink the formula that unlocked the abundance of the anointing.

One day while hanging out in San Diego, one of our interns named Philip asked if we could take him out street evangelizing. So my wife and I said, "Let's do it!" Philip was excited because he had just moved to San Diego to be an intern with us and had never seen a miracle released through his own hands and authority before. So the three of us waited upon the Lord and asked God for direction about where He wanted us to go. My wife Miranda received a word of knowledge about going to Starbucks, and about God wanting to heal someone with some sort of wrist brace on the right wrist. At the same time, I heard a word of knowledge about a place to go. I felt like the Lord was directing us to go to the Otay Ranch Mall and do evangelism there.

So we hopped in our car and headed first to Starbucks. When we got there, we decided to go through the drive-thru and ask the lady inside if anyone working there needed a miracle in their wrist. So we pulled up, ordered some lattes, and as we were at the window, Miranda asked the lady at the pick-up window if anyone needed a miracle.

The women said no. So we moved on to the Otay Ranch Mall in San Diego.

Sometimes you just have to step out in faith, even if it seems like you missed it.

We got to the mall and walked around. We felt led to go into Barnes and Noble's bookstore and evangelize there. So, in obedience to the inner prompting, we went in and started looking for people who the Lord would highlight to us to pray for. After about fifteen minutes of not really feeling like we found someone to pray for, we decided to leave. On the way out, while we passed through the foyer, we saw a woman standing there with her back to us. I felt led to spark up a conversation with her.

As she turned around to talk to us, we all noticed that she had a right wrist brace on. Just past her shoulder, we could see through the window of the foyer that there was a Starbucks in the Barnes and Noble bookstore. Even though it looked like we missed it at the Starbuck's drive-thru, we really hadn't. Here was the woman. There was the Starbucks. It all came together.

We ended up talking to her for quite some time and asked if we could pray for her. She said yes, so all three of us laid our hands on her, and she was instantly healed of severe pain from arthritis in her wrist. It was fun to see God move us along to a divine appointment that He had scheduled. The woman got totally encouraged that God loved her, and Philip saw his first miracle. But it didn't stop there.

After the miracle healing, we kept walking around the mall. In front of a Kay Jewelers store, we saw the manager and two sales representatives trying to get people to come inside and apply for a store credit card. As a perk, they were giving away free photo albums to anyone who would apply. So they stopped us and asked us if we would like to apply. We all noticed that one of the sales representatives had a soft cast on her left wrist. We said that we didn't want a credit card, but we *did* want to know what had happened to her wrist. She told us that she had fractured it the week before and that she was in serious pain because of the injury. So we told her the story of how we had just seen a woman in the bookstore get healed.

The manager got excited and thought that was a cool story. So we asked the girl if we could pray, and she said sure. We all three laid hands on her, commanded the pain to leave and the bone to be healed, and she felt a touch from God. Then we asked her to check it out to see if the pain was gone. As she did this, she started tearing up and said, "I can't believe this. All of the pain is gone." She took her soft cast off on the spot and showed us that she had regained full range of movement.

Just when we thought it couldn't get any better, the manager said, "I need a miracle in my body too. A year ago I broke my wrist, and it never healed right. There are bone spurs that have developed on my wrist that are very painful. Will it work on me too?" Then he shoved his wrist in our hands because he wanted prayer. So we prayed, and right there on the spot, Jesus healed him. They were both blown away by what God did for them that day. I ended up talking to them for about ten minutes about how God was showing them how much He loved them by healing them. It was an awesome encounter that was released by ascending the hill of the Lord and seeking Him as a team—then coming down off the mountain to release His Word to the ones He was sending us to. We needed to hear and obey to see the miracles. And the miracles seemed to multiply.

That is the abundance of the anointing—miracles multiply before your eyes.

And it is not just for a few, select disciples of Jesus who witness a transfiguration on a mountain. It is not just for a few who have mountaintop experiences in a meeting. It is for those who will accept the keys to the abundance—mixing up the formula, drinking it in, and letting the abundance fill them with joy. It is for those who know that they have been called to a higher purpose and calling—to be revivalists and evangelists to nations, to be those who have been with the Lord on the mountaintops and release Heaven's counsel and power to earth.

You, too, can come into an abundance of the anointing, but you must reach out for it and go after it. You can't just sit back, complacent and lazy, and wait for it to come to you.

God told Moses, "I am going to take you to a land filled with milk and honey." When the spies went into that land, they came out with reports of the fatness it contained—grapes the size of basketballs! Houses and fertile lands for the taking!

God doesn't want His Church to be in lack. Did you know there is a definition of poverty that goes way beyond money? There is poverty in the spirit that tells us we cannot have what we need. God does not want His Church to be without revelation anymore. God does not want His people to be without wisdom, knowledge, or the things of God so that we cannot do what we are called to do. The Bible says His people perish for lack of knowledge (see Hos. 4:6). Without knowledge, revelation, and fresh vision, we become complacent and lazy.

God wants to give us fresh vision. He wants to give us a blueprint so that we can stand on the mountain of God, hear His voice, and then be a voice for Him. If you want to be a revivalist, you need to start praying, taking time to be with God, and positioning yourself to have intimacy with God. If you do that, you will see Him in a new light and become transfigured into His likeness— the likeness of one who carries His Father's anointing in fullness and in joy.

The Key

The key to experiencing the abundance of the anointing is to delve into the Word until it becomes alive and powerful to you, sharper than a two-edged sword. As you take that sword out, the Holy Spirit brings revelation to you, and then through you, to others. The key involves the Word and the Spirit moving together in your life. How do you access that key? Invite the Holy Spirit to speak to you as you read the Bible.

Opening the Door

Holy Spirit, come as I sit and read the Word. Increase my understanding of what You are saying to me. Tell me more about You. Talk to me about the deeper truths embedded in Your Word. Then show me how to release Your Word to others. Soften my heart to hear You, and give me wisdom to know how to wield the sword of Your Word and truth to a lost and dying world.

CHAPTER 6

KEYS TO REVELATION

God wants to anoint you to have eyes to see and ears to hear so that you can perceive what He is doing around your life, your family, and your work place.

God wants to release to you a Spirit of Wisdom and Revelation in the knowledge of Him—because He wants you to know Him more. The Holy Spirit will reveal Jesus to you. He will reveal the Father to you. He will reveal Himself to you. He'll open up the Word of God and cause it to become real—so real that words will leap off the pages and become a reality in your heart as He begins to enlighten your eyes to see.

I was just in Seoul, Korea, with Bobby Conner for about eight days of awesome meetings, and during that time I had an experience where I went into a vivid trance. I watched as the hand of the Lord lifted up a torch. The fire that was in this torch mingled many different colors within it—beyond the ordinary reds and yellows you see in a flame.

Heavenly things are not like earthly things—colors and sights in Heaven are totally different from the way we see them on earth. What I saw was the most beautiful dark red flame mixed with a light blue flame—beautiful! I watched the Lord hold it out. And it was like He was saying, "Jerame, this is what I am making available in this place today if My people will embrace it." It was the torch of wisdom and revelation.

The color for wisdom is red, and the color for revelation is blue—and they go together. They are part of the seven spirits of God found in Isaiah 11:2 that refer to the anointing of God that would rest on Jesus. That anointing, which contains the Spirits of wisdom and understanding, counsel and might, knowledge and fear of the Lord, would rest upon Jesus, along with the Spirit of the Lord. God wants us to tap into wisdom and revelation because it causes us to come into deeper intimacy with God.

God wants you to come into the inner courts with Him; He wants you to taste and see that He is good. God wants to encounter you in that place and touch you by His Spirit. In that moment, you are changed and never the same.

That's revival.

Can you remember a defining moment when you had a personal encounter with God? Perhaps you went to a service and responded to an altar call because you felt the presence of God meeting you in that moment? Or perhaps you had a dream or vision or prophetic word that changed the face of who you are and caused you to go that much harder after God?

All of us have those kinds of moments. God wants us to have those kinds of moments, but not just once a year—God wants to lead us by His Spirit. God wants to draw us near to Him so that He can encounter us. We need ongoing encounters so that we do not fall into a place of complacence or familiarity. God wants to bring us into a place where our intimacy and love with Him are fiery hot. But that takes a supernatural encounter that we cannot work up on our own.

Many people think that dreams, visions, and encounters are what make us spiritual. God does not release revelation so that we can have a notch on our belt and make each other jealous. He gives us encounters so that we know more about His heart toward us or more about His Kingdom.

I have been in meetings all around the world when this revelatory realm comes into the room and the Lord begins to speak to me. He wants to release encounters to everyone. While the realms of Heaven open up for all, only a few enter in.

Trance Man

Once I was in Olympia, Washington, doing some revival meetings with a friend of mine named Jason Phillip. One night toward the end of the service, the Lord spoke to me and said that there was going to be a Maria Woodworth-Etter anointing for people to enter in to supernatural experiences with God. The Lord said, "I want you to release this anointing on the people at the end of the meeting, and I will begin to give people heavenly encounters." Some of you might be saying to yourselves, *Who is Maria Woodworth-Etter?* Maria Woodworth-Etter preached during the late 1800s and early 1900s. She was well-known for preaching in town squares; often, in the middle of her message, God would put her into a trance, and she would become as stiff as a board. Sometimes these trances would last an hour, and other times they would last three days. People would gather from all around to see this crazy lady who stood before them frozen, in a trance-like state.

Then, after a crowd would assemble around Maria, God would release her from the trance, and she would start preaching from where she left off as if nothing had even happened. Often, after she came out of these trances, she would preach the Gospel, and the Lord would do mighty signs and wonders in her meetings. One of the greatest signs that God released in her meetings was a corporate anointing of trances and revelation that would show up to confirm the preaching of the Word. There are documented times in her ministry when hundreds of people at the same time would fall into trances with God; they reported being taken to either Heaven or hell, receiving revelations from the Lord, and getting saved.

At the end of the meeting in Olympia, I stood up and began to declare that God was going to release an anointing in the room like Maria Woodworth-Etter carried. I told them that it was trance anointing, and some people were going to have heavenly encounters with God. Suddenly my spiritual eyes opened, and I saw a huge golden tornado come into the room. I began to prophesy the release of an Elijah-like realm of encounters in which God was going to take people up to Heaven in the whirlwind.

All of a sudden, many people in the room began to have experiences with God in visions. One man screamed loudly and fell to the ground and into a trance. About 30 minutes later, we closed out the meeting and went to the back room to talk and have some food. Meanwhile, the man who fell into a trance was still as stiff as a board. After we fellowshipped for some time, we all went back to my friend Jason's house to hang out. Three hours went by, and just as we were all about to go to bed, the phone rang. It was the wife of this man who fell into the trance at the meeting. She told Jason, "I don't know what to do. My husband is still as stiff as a board and hasn't moved once since the meeting." So my friend told her to bring her husband to his house. About half an hour later, the woman showed up with two other guys. They carried this man in and threw him on the couch; we noticed that the man was as stiff as a board. I had never seen anything like it before.

About an hour later, the man came out of the trance and was freaked out because he did not know where he was. He began to calm down as we talked to him, and then he told us of his experience. He had been crying out for more of God, when I began to prophesy that God was loosing a Maria Woodworth-Etter anointing for heavenly encounters and extended trances. He began to press into God. Then, just as I began to declare that there was a golden tornado that had come into the room to usher people into heavenly encounters, he saw it and was sucked up into it. As soon as he was taken up into this tornado, he met a man in the middle of the tornado, and that man was Jesus Christ. He had a face-to-face visitation with the Lord for over five hours in which the Lord showed and told him many things. When he came out of the vision, he found himself on the couch with all of us surrounding him and staring at him. The next weekend God began to birth this man into his ministry as he got invited to a church to share his face-to-face encounter. As he shared, many in the church got wrecked for God. Since this encounter, he has gone from being a volunteer worker at conferences to being in full-time ministry and pastoring a church in Olympia, Washington.

God wants to anoint you, too, to begin to have eyes to see and ears to hear, and a heart to perceive what He is doing in Heaven.

He wants you to have a revelation of who He is in your life and who you are as His sons and daughters, and as the Bride of Christ. The key to revelation is to know Him. Out of that knowing, you can release revelation to others. Your encounter can be transferred through you to them—just as trance man did when he spoke in that church immediately following his encounter.

God wants us to tap into the unseen realm. If we were to go to Heaven right now, what would it be like? What would it taste like? What would it smell like? What would it feel like? That's the realm that God wants to come into the earth. Often we put God in a box, and we have all of these preconceived notions of what it looks like for Heaven to invade earth. So many people only think of Heaven invading earth as it relates to signs, wonders, and miracles. That is only part of it; there is much more. God wants all of Heaven to invade our lives, especially through the realm of supernatural encounters, dreams, and visions.

Not Orphans

God wants us to understand that all things are possible with Him. He wants to change the way we think regarding our relationship with Him. Too many people think they have to *do* something to *get* something from God. God wants to crush the mentality of striving and release a greater revelation of His grace and love. We don't have to earn anything from God because Jesus went to the cross and declared, "It is finished." God has already given us everything regarding His kingdom. Ephesians 2:6 says that we are seated together in heavenly places with Jesus. God brought a new covenant to us, a covenant of the love of God. A lot of us haven't even wrapped our minds around the fact that we have a good Father in Heaven who longs to give good gifts to His children.

We are not orphans who have to beg for our needs. We don't have to try or strive to get things.

One woman who works with orphans has much to teach us about the orphan spirit. I remember listening to Heidi Baker talk about the kids at her orphanage in Mozambique. When children initially arrive at the Children's Center, poor, hungry, and unused to eating on a regular basis, they see the food set out on the table and go crazy. They jump on it and devour it. Even a month later, they are still jumping on it as if it will be their last meal. At first, Heidi asked the Lord what was going on with the children, and the Lord explained that they were not yet sons and daughters. The Lord said that they didn't understand that food was going to be there day after day because they never ate on a regular basis. They devoured everything they could quickly out of fear—because they didn't know when they would have their next meal.

That is the spirit of an orphan. By the time Heidi has had them for a couple of months, they know they are sons and daughters and that a meal is going to come every day. As they begin to come into a revelation of the Father's love through Rolland and Heidi Baker's ministry, they know that someone, Papa and Mama, is going to care for them.

We are much like the orphans of Mozambique. Many try to gobble up all they can—just for themselves. God wants us to stop acting like orphans running from conference to conference trying to devour everything we can. He wants to meet with you at your kitchen table, in your car, in your bedroom. He wants to meet with you wherever you will let Him meet with you. God especially wants to meet with you on the backside of the desert where you feel all alone.

The Key to Encountering God More Personally

Kenneth Hagin was an accurate prophet of God, and one of the most solid examples of longevity that we've seen in our time and day. He was a champion and a general in the Body of Christ, and whatever he put his hands to prospered. He was a man known for truth, faith, and revelation. He had the key to revelation. And I wanted to know how to get it.

When I was about a year and a half old in the Lord, I heard Hagin preach a message that revolutionized everything for me; it was about the secret to his success in ministry. It really was about the key to acquiring revelation.

He talked about how we need to pray Ephesians 1:17-18 over ourselves. In these verses, Paul prays for the Ephesians:

> *that the God of our Lord Jesus Christ, the Father of Glory, may give to you the spirit of wisdom and revelation in the knowledge of Him, the eyes of your understanding being enlightened; that you may know what is the hope of His calling, what are the riches of the glory of His inheritance in the saints.*

I took it to heart and put it into practice. I began to put my name in that Scripture, praying for myself something like this: "Lord, I am asking You to give me a spirit of wisdom. Give me a spirit of wisdom and revelation in the knowledge of You. Open the eyes of my heart, God, that I might know Your calling in my life and the inheritance that You have for Your Son and for me."

Every night before I would go to sleep I prayed that, and you know what happened? I began to have dreams, visions, and encounters with God. It wasn't a religious thing to me to pray that same prayer over and over again. I meant it with all my heart when I prayed this to God. What I was really saying was, "God, I really want to know You."

Paul the apostle prayed that prayer for the church of Ephesus, encouraging them to receive a spirit of wisdom and revelation in the knowledge of God. He prayed that the eyes of their hearts would be enlightened. The word *enlightened* means to be flooded with prophetic light. God wants us to have the eyes of our heart enlightened today and every day.

He wants you to have wisdom and revelation because He wants you to know Him more. And knowing Him releases authority to you and through you—the authority of being a son and a daughter. When you are carrying an experiential knowledge of who Christ Jesus is in your life and who He is around you, the devil becomes afraid of you—an ordinary person.

Paul was an ordinary man, but he was different from all of the other apostles. In fact, Paul was the one who was persecuting the Church. The thing that is amazing about Paul is that he never even traveled one day with Jesus in His earthly ministry. Nor was he taught by any of the other apostles. Yet he wrote more of the New Testament, saw more souls come into the Kingdom, and planted more churches than any of the other apostles did.

Paul didn't learn about Jesus from others; he was taught by God on the back side of the desert for ten years after he initially encountered God.

God wants to teach us things by His Spirit in the same way that He taught Paul. Paul wrote in Galatians 1:11-12,

> *I make known to you, brethren, that the gospel which was preached by me is not according to man. For I neither received it from man, nor was I taught it, but it came through the revelation of Jesus Christ.*

You see, Paul had a special relationship with God, and he had a special conversion too.

Jesus met him on the road to Damascus and knocked him off his horse with a laser beam from Heaven. This will disarm the theology that the Holy Spirit only shows up as a gentleman. How many of you know that God knows how to deal with every single person's heart? Some of us are more sensitive than others, and some of us have hard hearts. Some of us will stop and change direction when Jesus says, "Stop," and others need to be knocked off their high horse.

After Saul encountered the blinding light of Jesus, his natural eyes were blinded for three days. Then God sent Ananias to pray for him to receive his sight, as well as the Holy Spirit. When Ananias prayed for Saul, scales fell off of Saul's eyes, and he could see again (see Acts 9:18). Saul was renamed Paul, and his spiritual eyes were opened when his physical eyes were healed. He received a spirit of wisdom and revelation during that encounter that enabled him to learn more about Jesus and to become such friends with Him that they walked together in power for years to come.

God wants us to receive a spirit of wisdom and revelation so that we can walk in authority and power, too, taking dominion over powers, principalities, and spiritual hosts of wickedness in heavenly places. But we cannot walk alone. We must walk closely with Him. In fact, God wants to release to us four different things as we pray to receive the spirit of wisdom and revelation.

Four Things Wisdom and Revelation Will Do

Let's take a closer look at Ephesians 1:15-21. I want to break this part of Scripture down verse by verse and show you four things that you will receive as you begin to pray for the spirit of wisdom and revelation.

> *Therefore I also, after I heard of your faith in the Lord Jesus and your love for all the saints, do not cease to give thanks for you, making mention of you in my prayers: that the God of our Lord Jesus Christ, the Father of glory, may give to you the spirit of wisdom and revelation in the knowledge of Him, the eyes of your understanding being enlightened; that you may know what is the hope of His calling, what are the riches of the glory of His inheritance in the saints, and what is the exceeding greatness of His power toward us who believe, according to the working of His mighty power which He worked in Christ when He raised Him from the dead and seated Him at His right hand in the heavenly places, far above all principality and power and might and dominion, and every name that is named, not only in this age but also in that which is to come.*

The first thing that will happen as you begin to ask God for the spirit of wisdom and revelation is that He will anoint you to know Him more. In Ephesians 1:17, Paul prays that the Father of glory would give to the church a spirit of wisdom and revelation in the knowledge of Him. It's all about knowing Him, and He wants to anoint you to do it. The number one reason why God wants to give you the spirit of wisdom and revelation is so that you will know your Father in Heaven. The word *knowledge* in the Greek means "to know the precise and correct knowledge of who God is."[1] God the Father is raising up a Kingdom of sons and daughters who will know their Father in Heaven, and out of that place of authority, they will administrate His Kingdom in the earth.

The second thing that will happen is that God will begin to open your eyes to see in the spirit for the purpose of revealing your calling and destiny, as well as His future plans for His kingdom purposes in the earth. Ephesians 1:18 says, *"the eyes of your understanding being enlightened; that you may know what is the hope of His calling, what are the riches of the glory of His inheritance in the saints."* In this part of the Scripture, Paul prays that we would have the eyes of our understanding enlightened that we would know the hope of Jesus' calling, and His inheritance in the saints. When we as the Church begin to see Jesus' calling, and the purpose for which He came, we begin to understand ours. God wants the eyes of our understanding to be enlightened. In the Greek, *enlightened* means to have the eyes of our heart flooded with revelatory light.[2] When you begin to tap into the spirit of wisdom and revelation, and the eyes of your heart begin to be flooded with revelatory light, you will begin to have dreams, visions, and supernatural encounters with God that will reveal to you the plans of God in the earth. God sent Jesus as a model for us to know how we should walk as the sons and daughters of the Most High God. Jesus never did a thing unless He first saw what His Father in Heaven was doing (see John 5:19). God clearly wants us to see and understand the calling of Jesus because when we do, we will know who we are. When we can clearly see what our Papa is doing, we can do great exploits with Him.

The third thing that will happen as you receive the spirit of wisdom and revelation is that you will begin to tap into the raw power of God. Ephesians 1:19-20 says,

> *and what is the exceeding greatness of His power toward us who believe, according to the working of His mighty power, which He worked in Christ when He raised Him from the dead and seated Him at His right hand in the heavenly places.*

When you receive the spirit of wisdom and revelation, you will begin to tap into resurrection life and power. Paul knew about the resurrection power of God. In fact, he walked in more power than any of the other apostles did. If you want an increase of God's power in your life, start asking God for the spirit of wisdom and revelation.

The fourth and last thing I want to show you that will happen to the Church when we begin to receive the spirit of wisdom and revelation is that we will begin to walk, not just in the power of God, but also in the authority of God. Ephesians 1:21 says that Jesus is seated (as are we), "*far above all principality and power and might and dominion, and every name that is named, not only in this age but also in that which is to come.*" Our battle is not against flesh and blood, but against powers and principalities and spiritual hosts of wickedness in heavenly places (see Eph. 6:12). How many of you know that Jesus defeated the enemy once and for all when He said it was finished? God wants us to understand that we are seated together with Christ in heavenly places (see Eph. 2:6), and that He is the head of the Church. If Jesus is the head, and we are His Body, and God has made the enemy Jesus' footstool, then that means the devil is under our feet too.

I believe that we are entering into a season when God is going to show us things through the spirit of wisdom and revelation in dreams and visions, so that we can have victory over the devil and take back the land we live in for Jesus. In the first chapter, I told a story of how God burned to the ground a hotel that was overtaken by drug dealers, pimps, and prostitutes. After we followed the leading of a dream that I had the night before, which told us to sing the song of the Lord over that region, God released this great sign in the natural of something He dealt with in the spirit realm that opposed His Kingdom. As we, the Church, were obedient to the simple instructions that came by the wisdom of God, He destroyed the stronghold of lust and perversion in that city. God wants us as a Church to begin to tap into the spirit of wisdom and revelation so that we can have total victory over the enemy and see His Kingdom established in our nation.

God wants us to understand what it is to have true intimacy with Him. If you study Galatians, you'll read that Paul didn't even go see Peter, John, or any of the other apostles for a number of years. Face to face, God taught Paul on his own. And when he was ready, he went out carrying the glory and revelation of Jesus Christ so strongly that the apostles Peter and John—being the superstar guys that they were in the Church at that time—looked at him and said, "You've got something crazy. We're commissioning you to go reach the Gentiles." They saw the anointing and authority on Paul.

I love that those apostles weren't prideful. They saw what was inside of Paul and released him into the ministry God called him to. They said, "Man, you didn't even walk with us when we were with Jesus, but you've got more revelation than we do."

How did Paul gain so much revelation? Paul, on the back side of the desert with the Lord, ended up giving us a clue when he wrote, "Whether I was in the body or out of the body, I do not know..." (see 2 Cor. 12:2). He was somewhere with God—out of sight of men. Paul was lifted up time after time to be with Jesus. Of all the signs, wonders, miracles, and supernatural things I've seen, my heart longs the most for personal encounters with Jesus alone. My heart longs the most to have experiences with Daddy because when that happens, I am supernaturally transformed on the inside. Whether I understand the encounter or not, there's a deposit of Heaven put right inside of me that changes the DNA of who I am and causes me to become more like God.

God wants to activate us to a new level of knowing Him. I want you to see this because here's the deal—the wisdom and revelation of God is birthed in the desert. Paul was taught on the back side of the desert. And so are we. The desert is a place of personal encounter.

The desert is a place that is hot. It is also a place of encountering God's fire. When we become more like Jesus, there is an exchange that takes place.

Remember the torch of wisdom and revelation I saw the Lord lifting up? We need to step into the fire in order to receive it. I've been going through the fire for about eight years. Did you know that when you get saved you step into that realm?

And do you know what the fire does? It's the fire mentioned in Malachi 3:2-3—it comes to purge, burn, and remove all that's in you that's not of God.

How are we going to receive this wisdom and revelation? Paul received his training in the desert, in a place of hiding. Do you ever feel that way? Hidden, unrecognized, nobody seeing you for who you are? God may have you in the desert because the fire of God needs to touch all the motives and intents of your heart, everything that's in there that's not of God. He wants us to embrace His fire because when we do, it will change us. God also wants to burn out all the bondages, limitations, and hindrances that keep us from truly stepping into more with Him. He wants to break that yoke of fear over your life. He wants to break off the insecurities that you have. He wants to break the strongholds that the enemy has put in your life, that have stopped you from becoming the man or woman of God you are called to be. He does this through the fire of God. He is holding out a torch and inviting you to enter in. The way into greater revelation is to accept the fire.

God wants us to understand that seasons of fire change our hearts toward Him so that we know Him more. Many churches in the nations out there value the power of God above everything. They can minister in power, but they are a bunch of anointed jerks—they lack love. They move in power, but their churches are a mess, their families are a mess, and that's not the fruit of God's anointing. It seems like they never knew the Father. They are orphans who want to be somebodies. It takes a son to become a father, and it takes a father to produce a son. We need to know Him more...not grab for more. But be content to live in the fire for a while on the back side of the desert...just to be with Him.

God wants you to pray that you will receive the spirit of wisdom and revelation—and the key to revelation is relationship with Him.

Moses was much like Paul. He had an encounter with the fire of God's wisdom and revelation on the back side of the desert and was forever changed. As he encountered the wisdom and revelation of God in the form of a burning bush, he went from being like an orphan to knowing who he was, and understanding his destiny. Remember, the wisdom and revelation of God will bring you into the knowledge of Him, as well as release to you the understanding of your calling.

In Exodus 3, we read that Moses was tending the flock of Jethro, his father-in-law, the priest of Midian, and he led the flock to the back side of the desert. Eventually, he came to Horeb, the mountain of God, where the *"Angel of the Lord appeared to him in a flame of fire from the midst of a bush. So he looked, and behold, the bush was burning with fire, but the bush was not consumed"* (Exod. 3:2). When the Lord saw that Moses had turned aside to look at the bush, He called to him from the midst of the bush.

He said, *"Do not draw near this place. Take your sandals off your feet, for the place where you stand is holy ground"* (Exod. 3:5).

I want you to see this: Moses is wandering around the back side of the desert. How many of you feel like you are just wandering around the desert, going from one place to the next, not knowing where you are going? Maybe you feel like you have been in the desert running around in circles with a bunch of sheep. God wants you to clearly hear His voice. It was as Moses *turned aside* to see or embrace the fire of God that God began to speak to him and make Himself known to Moses. God then began to tell Moses about his destiny as a deliverer to bring the children of Israel out of the land of Egypt.

If you want to hear the voice of God, embrace His fire—the wisdom and revelation of God. Allow Him to come into your life. The fire will burn away all that stops you from hearing and seeing Him. After Moses embraced the fire, God began to give him revelation about his destiny and calling.

God wants to birth a generation of no compromise and purity, a generation who is on fire for God, a generation who encounters Him. The generation that is coming is extreme and radical, and if we don't give them a taste of the real thing, of genuine encounter with God's presence and power, they will turn to the dark side. A Gospel without demonstration and power, without a God of love, is meaningless to them.

God wants to set you on fire so you can set others on fire. God wants that torch in His hand to be you— so that everywhere you go you begin to set people on fire. Your life is an example. Have you ever been around somebody, and you know they have something that you don't have? And so you become jealous for it? God wants you to be that person—carrying the same revelation of God's personal love and revelation. God doesn't call the qualified; He uses the foolish things of this world to confound the wise. He even uses you and me.

God wants you to know Him more. He longs to meet you in the desert and release to you the spirit of wisdom and revelation about who He is and who He can be through you. You need only ask your Father for it. Orphans don't ask Daddy for anything because they don't know He exists. But we do. We have a good Daddy who gives good gifts to those who ask (see Matt. 7:11; James 1:17).

Several things will begin to happen as you pray, "Lord, give me the spirit of wisdom and revelation."

God will begin to open up your spirit to know Him beyond an intellectual level—spirit-to-Spirit contact that changes you as you see Him. He wants you to behold Him as in a mirror, face to face, and as you do, you will go from glory to glory and be transformed. I call it the great exchange.

When His presence comes, there is an exchange to be made. And it is made in the fire, in the place of hiding, as you come into an awareness of how personally He loves you.

He wants to give you something that you didn't earn. He wants to give you something that you didn't pay the price for. He wants to give you something that you don't have to strive for, for He wants to give you His love.

He manifests His love by giving you the desires of your heart. Desire Him first—and, because He loves you, you will enter into the realm of His manifest presence. If you want to have visions, dreams, experiences, and all these things, you will have them.

Test God to see if His Word is real.

Pray Ephesians 1:17 over yourself and watch what happens.

The Key

The key to increased revelation is by accessing the spirit of wisdom and revelation. In Ephesians 1:17, Paul prays that the Father of glory would give the Church a spirit of wisdom and revelation in the knowledge of Him. It's all about knowing Him, and He wants to anoint you to do it. The number one reason why God wants to give you the spirit of wisdom and revelation is so that you will know your Father in Heaven. The word *knowledge* in the Greek means "to know the precise and correct knowledge of who God is." God the Father is raising up a Kingdom of sons and daughters who will know their Father in Heaven, and out of that place of authority administrate His Kingdom in the earth.

Opening the Door

Lord, I am asking You to give me a spirit of wisdom. Give me a spirit of wisdom and revelation in the knowledge of You. Open the eyes of my heart, God, that I might know Your calling in my life, that I might know the inheritance that You have for Your Son and for me. God, I really want to know You.

Endnotes

1. See http://www.studylight.org/lex/grk/ view.cgi?number=1922; *epignosis:* "precise and correct knowledge of things ethical and divine."

2. See http://www.studylight.org/lex/grk/ view.cgi?number=5461; *photizo*: "to give light, to shine."

CHAPTER 7

KEYS TO POWER AND MIRACLES

In the fall of 2003, I was attending Sonoma State University in California where I played baseball on the college team and was heavy into the college party scene. I had grown up partying and playing baseball. I had started using and drinking at the age of thirteen. Despite being in college, binge drinking, recreational drug use, and going out to party was still a regular thing for me. The only thing that kept me from going off the deep end was playing baseball with a dream of going pro.

One day I hit rock bottom. After many nights of partying in a row, I thought about the way I was living and started questioning what I was doing. At this point, I didn't want to smoke weed and drink alcohol anymore. I realized that partying five days a week was not going to help me accomplish my professional goal. So out of my own strength I started trying to quit. I would go about a week without smoking or drinking and then would fall right back into it again because of my friends. It was a terrible feeling. I was unable to enjoy partying with my friends anymore: I wanted to be with them, but I wanted to be away from them because I felt the partying undermined my dream.

Still unable to quit partying and conflicted about life, I went home to Colorado where I grew up for Christmas break. As soon as I hooked up with my old friends, it was off to the fiesta.

Then one night my mom, who was a Christian, asked me to go to church with her in the morning. Mom had been a Christian for years. In fact, she was the only Spirit-filled Christian in our entire family—on both my father's and mother's side. Everyone considered her a Jesus freak. Throughout my whole life she would preach at me. But I would listen to her because I had witnessed God do a miracle in her life. When I was thirteen, she had breast cancer so badly that she lost all of her hair and was close to dying. Then someone gave her a Bible, and she read it and saw that Jesus healed people. So out-loud she said, "God, if You are really real, then heal me." Then she fell into a vision. The hand of God touched her, and she was instantly healed of breast cancer. Because of this event I knew God was real; I just didn't want to follow Him.

When my mom asked me to go to church that night, I only said yes because I knew it would make her happy. So when church rolled around in the morning, I found myself on the very back row with my family. I was thinking, "OK, all I have to do is sit through this boring service, get it over with; she's happy, and we can go home."

God decided to capture my attention during the service. After the worship was over, the pastor asked, "Who here wants to be in the big leagues?"

Then he began to preach the Gospel and related it to baseball. He started saying that if we wanted to live in Heaven, which is the big leagues, we have to accept Jesus in the minor leagues, which was this life. He said that just like in the natural a player has to do well in the minor leagues of baseball to get to the big leagues. This spoke to me big time. So at the end of the meeting I walked up to the pastor and said hello. Then I took out of my coat pocket a real Major League baseball that I carried with me everywhere I went and gave it to him. He looked at the ball, recognized what it was, and said, "This is a major league baseball; I just gave a major league sermon."

Then I told him that I played baseball at a college in California, and that my dream was to be a pro baseball player.

His response made me want to give my life to Jesus. He said, "God can use you in the pros! In fact, I want you to sign this ball for me, and I'm going to be the first one to have your signature before you go to the pros." So I signed the ball, handed it to him, and left with my family. Later that day, while by myself in my room, I gave my life to the Lord. No one lead me in a prayer; I just gave my life to Him.

When I did this, I said to Jesus, "Lord, I want You to come into my heart today. But I don't want to be like all of the hypocrites that are out there that say they are living for You, but aren't. In fact, this is how it's going to be. Just as hard as I have run into the darkness my whole life, I want to run into the light. Come into my life now."

That was it. I didn't feel any goose bumps or hear angels singing. I just made a commitment to Jesus and decided that I was going to run as hard as I could after Him. I went to sleep that night feeling nothing special, but I woke up on fire for God and have never stopped since. I experienced total freedom from the desire to do drugs and drink alcohol and became an even bigger Jesus freak than my mom.

It is not enough to just have a testimony of salvation, catch fire, and smolder out. God wants you to know Him more and more, to go on to other encounters that keep the fire burning.

The other night I was on a walk with the Lord, and He said this to me, "Jerame, I want you to tell My people that I want them to know Me. No longer do I want them to put Me in a box and compartmentalize Me. I want them to know every facet of Me."

Lots of people love Jesus and believe they know Jesus, but they don't know the Father. And there are a lot of people who know the Father, but they don't know the Holy Spirit. God wants you to begin to experience every facet of who He is. He wants you to know Him as all three parts of the Godhead: The Father, Son, and Holy Spirit.

God wants to leave that revelation up to us. He wants to open up the revelation to us that the Holy Spirit is the one with us here on the earth now; Jesus is ruling and reigning at the right hand of God; the Father is ruling and reigning in Heaven. The Kingdom of God is within you. But God wants to take you to a deeper place—into a relationship with the Holy Spirit—because it's the Holy Spirit who Jesus said He would send to His disciples. He told them that it was better for them that He went away. You know, they probably thought that was a crazy statement. *What do you do mean, it is better for us that You go away, Jesus? Come on, You're the most anointed guy anybody has ever seen! You're the Savior of the world!* He knew they didn't understand.

He was saying to them, "It's better for you that I go away because the Paraclete, the Comforter, the Helper will come to you. And this Holy Spirit will tell you about things to come and remind you of all that I have said and will do" (see John 16:13). The Holy Spirit is the essence of His love resident on the earth today.

It is not enough to have a one-time experience of meeting Jesus and giving your life to Him. He wants you to come into an encounter with the Holy Spirit that is His manifest presence—His love made manifest to you.

I remember the first time I encountered the manifest love of God. It was late one night in 2004 at around 4 A.M. while reading a book by Benny Hinn, called *Good Morning, Holy Spirit*. I was reading about how Benny had gone to a Kathryn Kuhlman meeting in Pittsburgh and received an impartation of the Holy Spirit. After this impartation, the Holy Spirit begins to visit him in his room at home. As I read this book, I was becoming hungrier for more of God. Eventually, I got to this place in the book where Benny wrote about how he would just lock himself away in his room and say, "Come, Holy Spirit," and he felt the warm blanket of God's presence and love wrap itself around him. At one point, Benny said that all he would do is call on the Holy Spirit and He would come.

So I put the book down and decided to try this myself. I closed my eyes and said to the Lord, "Father, I'm Your son just like Benny. I want Your presence to come on me like a wet blanket of love, too. Holy Spirit, come!" Then all of a sudden this warm, liquid love like a blanket came upon my body as I was lying on my bed. It was the most euphoric thing that I had ever experienced before in my life. I just lay there and felt like I was vibrating in the bed—every nerve ending sensing the Holy Spirit. Then I kind of got scared, and said, "Stop!"

Right when I said this, the blanket of God's love lifted. Then I realized that I didn't want it to stop, nor did I want to quench the Holy Spirit. So I said to the Father, "If this is really You, let it happen again." I felt the warm blanket of God's love fall on me again. Then I knew it was God and wanted it to continue. This experience lasted about one hour and launched me into a two-year season of hungering to be in God's presence.

I wanted God more than I wanted to party with my friends. However, I still wanted to be a pro baseball player. I dreamed of being a pro baseball player, and God had even given me a promise that he would use me for His glory in the big leagues.

Three years later, God was faithful to fulfill that dream and give me the desire of my heart. I was offered a contract to play independent league professional baseball in Texas. Around that same time, I had begun to go on short-term mission trips all around the world—to places like India, Mexico, and even Africa. When I went on these trips, I experienced lots of awesome things. I had seen many notable, remarkable miracles, such as cripples walking, deaf hearing, blind seeing, and much more. My heart began to turn more toward God's Kingdom. I longed to be with my Father, doing what He was doing, being with Him.

I was still playing baseball and training in the off-season to get ready for my first year of pro baseball when on my way to Africa on the plane, God began to speak to me about what He wanted me to do in life. I will never forget what happened. I was reading a book called *The Final Quest*. As I was reading this book, the Lord began to speak to me out of the blue about the topic of baseball.

He said to me, "Son, I am a good God, and I give My people the desires of their heart, and I have been faithful to give you the desire of your heart with baseball. I want you to know something. Baseball is your dream for your life, but it's not mine."

Then he said, "My dream for your life is that you would preach the Gospel to the nations, not play baseball."

I was shocked.

He spoke again and said, "Jerame, if you are willing to give up your dreams to live Mine, you will be rich in the things of the Kingdom, and you will see My power. And if you are not, I am such a good God, I will bless your baseball career, and you will still be successful and play in the big leagues and be able to finance My Kingdom."

It took me about two minutes to consider what I had just heard. I didn't want to play baseball anymore if that wasn't God's highest plan for my life. And so I laid down baseball to pursue preaching. Then the Lord opened doors for me, and I ended up getting invited to travel with many amazing fathers and mothers in the spirit who were all preaching the Gospel—men and women like Todd Bentley, Bobby Conner, Keith Miller, and Patricia King, and many others. Within about two years from this call to quit baseball and enter into ministry, I was released into full-time ministry and started traveling all around the world. Because of the intimate relationship I had been developing with the Lord, getting to know Him and His ways, God started releasing His revelation and power through me in ways that constantly amaze me.

Doing the Stuff

One time I was in Nashville, Tennessee, speaking at a conference and ministering. During the worship, the Lord opened my spiritual eyes, and I began to get words of knowledge for healing. As the intensity of the worship increased, in a vision I watched as the glory of God began to touch a woman. I saw the glory of God go into the nostrils of her nose, and I heard the Lord say that there was someone in the meeting who had lost their sense of smell. As a result of that vision, when I got up to minister that night, I just simply called out what I saw in the spirit to a crowd of about 300 people. Sure enough, there was one woman who had completely lost her sense of smell. As she came forward, I boldly told the people in the meeting, "Tonight God is going to restore what the devil stole from this woman and give her a sense of smell back."

Then we laid hands on her and prayed for her. After we prayed, I asked if anyone in the crowd had any anointing oil so we could test the miracle out. Finally someone brought me a small flask of aromatic oil, and I asked the woman, "Would you have been able to smell this oil before I prayed for you?"

She answered, "No, it would have been impossible. I have not had a sense of smell for over a year."

I took the oil, put it under her nose, and asked her if she could smell the oil. Instantly, tears ran down her face, and she cried out, "I'm healed!"

The Lord spoke to me again, prompting me to tell the people that this miracle was a prophetic sign that God is restoring that which the devil had stolen from the churches in this region. He was restoring discernment to His Church; the sense of smell speaks about the gift of discernment.

One of the keys to walking in power and miracles is that we need to listen to Him and trust what He is speaking. We learn about what God is doing as we step out and do the stuff with Him.

I was in Dudley, England, speaking at meetings that have become known as the Dudley outpouring. In this meeting, the Lord spoke to me about giving an altar call for the healing of those who had injuries that resulted in metal plates, pins, and screws being surgically inserted. He told me that if I gave an altar call for those with metal in their bodies, He would do creative miracles. In obedience, I gave the altar call. Three people came forward.

The first was a woman in her sixties who had a metal rod in her left hip inserted over five years ago. I stalled for a moment, silently asking the Lord how He wanted me to pray for this woman. Then He spoke to me, "I want you to dance with her. If you dance with her, I will completely heal her."

I said to the woman, "Here is how we are going to pray. I'm going to dance with you, and God is going to heal you completely."

I took the woman by the hand and began to dance with her. As I did this, the power of God came upon the woman, and she fell out onto the floor. After about thirty seconds, the woman stood up completely healed.

I asked her how she knew that God has healed her and asked her to try to do something that she could not do before.

The woman said, "It was impossible for me to lie down on my left side where the metal rod was inserted. I have not been able to sleep on my left side since the operation because of the discomfort of the metal in my hip." So I told her to test her healing out by lying down on her left side in the meeting. When she did this, for the first time in over five years, she was able to lie down on her left side without excruciating pain from the metal in her hip. It was an awesome creative miracle that the Lord did for her. She then began to feel for the metal rod and could not find it anymore.

The miracle was awesome, but the testimony about what happened prior to the miracle and prayer was even more powerful than the miracle itself. The night after this amazing miracle happened, a different woman came up and said, "I have to give a testimony about what happened last night. I am a friend of the woman who God healed last night with the metal rod in her hip. My friend was so in awe about what God did that she forgot to tell you something very significant about the miracle that took place." This woman had driven her friend to the meeting in faith that she would be healed. Before they got to the meeting, they both prayed and agreed on the miracle. The woman prayed in the car, "Lord, would You heal me so I can dance again?"

Another key to releasing the healing miracles of God is this: God is a creative God who moves in odd ways—not because of our great faith and anointing—but because He loves the one He is ministering to. If you are going to move in miracles, you must move in His love.

Sometimes His love reaches out to those who not only do not know Him, but who seek to work against Him. God loves even those we think are less likely candidates for miracles.

I was on vacation with a friend in Florida, and one night my friend and I decided to relax in the hotel's hot tub. As we did, the Lord began to speak to me about a woman who was in the hot tub with us. He told me that she was a spiritual woman, and He wanted me to witness to her. In obedience, I started a conversation with her and actually asked her if she was spiritual. It turned out that she was, and she talked for a long time about all kinds of strange spiritual experiences she'd had!

Then she asked me what I believed. I told her I was a Christian and I believed in Jesus. Immediately she started laughing and making fun of me. So I began to tell her how the power of God healed the deaf and blind people when I was in India. No matter. She just kept on mocking Jesus and saying God had no power.

As it was getting late, the owner of the hotel came by and said our time was up in the hot tub. But before we left, the Lord put it on my heart to ask the woman if we could pray for her. She said OK, but she wanted us to know that she was an avid student of the black arts and the occult, and we learned that she was a witch. No problem. I just told her, "So what! Let me pray for you. I'm not afraid of you." Then she allowed my friend and me to pray for her. I took one hand, and my friend took the other, but she said, "No, only one of you at a time. I want to be able to center all my energy on one of you." I said that was OK, gave her my hand, and began to pray.

Immediately I went into the visions of God and saw a picture of a rose and began to prophesy to her what I saw. I told the woman that God loved her, and from a heavenly perspective, He saw her as beautiful as a rose even though she didn't know Him. I went on to say that He saw her as beautiful because He created her in beauty in her mother's womb. At that exact moment, the power of God whacked this witch, and she began to scream out loud, "You're blocking my powers; you're blocking my powers! No one has ever blocked my powers before!"

I answered: "That's because Jesus is the greatest power there is!" The power of God was absolutely overwhelming this woman.

Next, I turned to my friend and said, "Now you pray for her."

As he did, I silently asked God if I could throw a fireball upon the woman. The Lord gave me a clear *yes*. So I threw a fireball at her—silently, by faith. And when I did, the power of God hit her and knocked her back several feet. Then she started screaming, "What is this energy? I have never felt any thing like it before."

I told her, "That's the Holy Spirit!"

She immediately ran off screaming. She felt God's authentic power—a greater love than she had ever known—and she could not handle it. Who knows the final outcome? Sometimes, we don't get to hear the end of the story.

No matter what happens, the key to moving in power is this: just do it! Do what you hear the Father saying.

Some of you are probably wondering if my friends and I are special people—especially called and anointed of God. I believe that God is calling you, too, to step out in authority, love, and power. We are all sons and daughters of a heavenly Father with all the rights to inheritance in the natural and in the supernatural.

Some of you are confused about what you are called to do, or about where God is calling you to go. You are like Moses, still wandering the desert, stumbling upon the burning bush.

God wants you to move beyond just staring at the burning bush. He wants you to realize that today you are standing on holy ground.

God spoke to Moses at the burning bush and the first thing He said was, *"Take the sandals off of your feet, for you are standing on holy ground."* (See Exodus 3:5.) Holy ground is the place of destiny. God began to speak to Moses about the very thing that He had in mind for him—plans that were in His heart before time even began.

He said, "Moses, I have heard My people cry in the land of Egypt about their oppression and the torment with which their taskmasters have afflicted them. I want you to set them free."

Moses wasn't exactly excited about this news. In fact, I don't think Moses was secure enough at that moment to receive it. Have you ever received a word from God and your first thought was, "That's just too much"? God wants to stretch us.

He wants us to understand that what is impossible for us is possible with Him. If you could do something that was possible in your own strength, gifts, and talents, where would your faith be? Why would you need faith? Moses didn't say, "Yes, Lord, let's go take the nations!" He replied, "Lord, how are they even going to believe that You sent me?"

God made a way. He created a strategy for the deliverance of a nation, gave it to Moses, partnered him with Aaron and Miriam, and said, "Go for it!" Moses accepted the call to destiny despite his fear. He moved in obedience, trusting that God would not let Him down.

God can move alone to deliver nations, yet He calls us into the privilege of working with Him—sons and daughters working alongside Papa. He is calling you, too.

In Singapore, some of the most famous pastors that we work with tell amazing stories about Muslims being saved supernaturally. I've got a Muslim friend who had a dream that Jesus came and preached the Gospel to him personally, and he got saved. That's a regular occurrence in Asia and in different regions of the world where there is high-level persecution against Muslims who convert to Christianity. There are places where the Gospel may not be accepted, but it doesn't stop God. And God is inviting us to go and release His supernatural revelation and power. God doesn't need us to go and preach; if we are not willing, He'll do it Himself. But here's the invitation: we get to go with Him.

God wants to extend the anointing for miracles, signs, and wonders through us. But first, we have to be hearing His voice and moving in obedience to what He asks us to do.

Once I was in Cedar Rapids, Iowa, doing some meetings where the Lord had me preaching on overcoming the fear of the supernatural. As the message came to an end, the spirit of prophecy fell upon me, and I began to prophesy as the Spirit of God led. I declared that God was going to release the wisdom and revelation of God, and that He was going to push out of that region a religious spirit that held back people from entering into the deep things of God.

Then I declared, "From this night on, more supernatural experiences will take place in this city than ever before. God is going to release Elijah-like experiences and encounters."

It sounded a little crazy, but the words just seemed to be flowing out of my mouth freely. As a sign that this word of the Lord was true, I continued, many people and religious leaders who lived in the area, and who had opposed the supernatural, would begin to have Damascus road experiences. God would invade their lives and reveal Himself to them in a supernatural way.

The Spirit of God lifted from me after I made the declaration, so I handed the microphone to the pastor who closed the service down. Within about half an hour of that declaration, a man and a couple of his friends who were driving into Cedar Rapids had an incredible experience. They noted the time and the place where they were just a second before the heavens opened, and they were caught up into something they didn't believe in.

All of a sudden, two chariots of fire appeared to them in the natural, right outside of their car on the highway—one swooping down on either side of the car. Immediately, they all fell into a trance and blacked out for about two minutes.

When they came to, they noted that their car clock read two minutes later than when the experience began. Then, they passed a landmark in the city that was forty-two miles from the place where the chariots of fire appeared to them. The Lord gave them this Elijah-like experience and transported them forty-two miles in two minutes.

The man who had been driving the car showed up the next night to my meeting to testify about this experience. After the meeting, the pastor at the church told me that this man had been speaking against the supernatural and a lot of other things in his church. His testimony was the sign in the natural that the supernatural things of God would begin to happen in that city. It was a confirmation of the declaration I had spoken the night before.

Why speak against the supernatural ways of God? He is way bigger than you. In fact, He is calling you, too, to enter into the deeper things of God and to take hold of the keys to power and miracles.

In this season of God's manifest presence and power, we need to be open to move beyond a simple but profound initial encounter of salvation. That is merely the introduction to Jesus and the Kingdom. He wants you to move into ongoing encounters with His love, His Manifest Presence, and the Holy Spirit. And He invites you to move with Him to release Heaven on earth through miracles, signs, and wonders. This invitation is for anyone who will receive it.

God is calling you to join the revolutionaries who will release a revolution of God's love and power to a desperate world.

Will you come?

Something *big* is beginning to happen all around the world. And we want you to be a part of it.

The Key

The key to increased power and anointing for miracles is to know the love of God, to trust that you are walking in His love, and to be willing to give His love away. You need ongoing encounters of the love of God to refresh and fill you in this world. You also need to know that He loves you just because He created you—not for what you do. You cannot earn His love. And you can only give away what He first gives to you. So lock yourself in your room and wait actively—asking the Holy Spirit to come.

Opening the Door

Father, I'm your son just like Benny Hinn and your daughter just like Kathryn Kuhlman. I want Your presence to come on me like a wet blanket of love, too. Holy Spirit, come!

Chapter 8

OPENING THE DOORS TO THE REVOLUTION OF LOVE

I've talked a lot about keys in this book and shared some amazing God stories. By now, some of you may be wondering—*Hey! What are the keys for?* Simply put, the keys unlock the doors to relationship with Jesus and revelation from the Holy Spirit. Out of your deepening intimacy with God, you ultimately use the key to authority that unlocks the door to a revolution of love that will change the world. But let's recap all of the keys I've been talking about so you can see the complete picture of what is about to take place in the world and why God wants you to access these keys and unlock these doors.

In the first chapter I talked about an angel handing me two keys: the key of David in Isaiah 22 and the keys to the Kingdom referenced in Matthew 16.

The first key the angel revealed is the key of David written about in Isaiah 22:22. Isaiah 22:22-23 states,

> *The key of the house of David I will lay on his shoulder; So he shall open, and no one shall*

> *shut; And he shall shut, and no one shall open.*
> *I will fasten him as a peg in a secure place,*
> *and he will become a glorious throne to his*
> *father's house.*

The second key is referred to in Matthew 16:17-19 where Jesus says,

> *Blessed are you, Simon Bar-Jonah, for flesh*
> *and blood has not revealed this to you, but*
> *My Father who is in heaven. And I also say*
> *to you that you are Peter, and on this rock*
> *I will build My church, and the gates of hell*
> *shall not prevail against it. And I will give*
> *you the keys of the kingdom of heaven, and*
> *whatever you bind on earth will be bound in*
> *heaven, and whatever you loose on earth will*
> *be loosed in heaven.*

These two keys are the keys to intimacy and authority. Both keys speak about intimacy with Jesus releasing authority on earth—through *you!* David and Peter both experienced closeness with Jesus beyond their peers. It wasn't their giftedness and talents that God loved about them; He loved that they loved Him. God is a God of relationship. He values being with you. And out of the time you spend with Him, you get to know Him and His ways, and become so like Him that you move in the authority that is released to sons and daughters of the King.

Intimacy leads to authority—but you need to walk closely with the Holy Spirit and access revelation before you act in your authority. Most of the stories I've written about speak of the revelation we need to enter into so that we can move into our personal destinies.

Most of this book focuses on the third key, initially referred to in Luke 11:52: *"Woe to you lawyers! For you have taken away the key of knowledge. You did not enter in yourselves, and those who were entering in you hindered."* That key of knowledge is revelatory knowledge...not intellectual knowledge. Jesus is inviting you to come up higher and access the revelatory realms of Heaven, to know Him, to hear Him, to see Him, and to come into supernatural experiences that should become part of your ordinary Christian experience.

The three main keys—intimacy, authority, and revelation—unlock the doors to intimacy, authority, and revelation. And as we unlock these doors, we will see that Jesus is leading us someplace specific...into the inner courts of His counsel where He tells us what is to come.

And something *big* is coming. Do you want to be part of it?

First, you need to make the supernatural encounters of revelation part of your experience. I gave several keys to this in previous chapters:

- Reach out and grab the keys others possess, learning from the revelation of those who are moving in supernatural ministry today and in the past.

- Seek after the spirit of counsel and might. Learn to hear and obey as you step out and do what the Holy Spirit prompts you to do.

- Talk about God stories and discover how that opens portals to further revelation. It builds faith, and God moves in response to faith—because He delights to reveal more of Himself to His daughters and sons!

- Hunger after God and climb up the mountain into His glory realm. Hanging out with Him is the key to accessing the abundance of the anointing.

- Know that you are not an orphan but have a spiritual inheritance you can access as a son or daughter. Let the understanding of who you are in Him enable you to boldly ask for the spirit of wisdom and revelation. This leads you into knowing God in many different ways—as Father, Son, and Holy Spirit—and in greater intimacy.

- Go beyond the initial stage of meeting God and move into your destiny in this hour. He wants you to move into ongoing encounters with His love, His Manifest Presence, and the Holy Spirit. And He invites you to move with Him to release Heaven on earth through miracles, signs, and wonders. This invitation is for anyone who will receive it.

Then, you need to know that Jesus wants you to come along with Him and pass through the doors of destiny. *What are the keys for?* They unlock the doors to relationship and revelation—and ultimately unlock the authority you carry to release a revolution of love that will change the world.

The Doors

If you want to come closer to Jesus, come! Jesus holds the door open to you anytime! Luke 11:10 says, *"For everyone who asks receives, and he who seeks finds, and to him who knocks it will be opened."* Pursue God. He is always holding open the door to relationship with you. And He is always inviting you to ask boldly for what you need, to do what He is calling you to do. Do you need wisdom? Ask and He will deposit in your brain just the right strategy to shift the situation that puzzles you. Do you need revelation? Ask and He will send His angel, or a dream, or a vision to you to tell you what is to come, or what to do, or where to go.

Since God loves you, He will come when you invite Him. You can open the door to Jesus and invite greater fellowship! Revelation 3:20 says, *"Behold, I stand at the door and knock. If anyone hears My voice and opens the door, I will come in to him and dine with him, and he with Me."* Sharing a meal with someone speaks of deeper relationship and intimacy. But you need to open the door, turn your attention to Jesus, and spend time with Him. He is always willing. Are you?

Out of your relationship, there will be special times of encounter that Jesus initiates in which He tells you of things to come—not just for another person, or for a particular meeting that you may be speaking at, but for the whole nation...or even the world. Revelation 4:1 speaks about this: *"After these things I looked, and behold, a door standing open in heaven. And the first voice which I heard was like a trumpet speaking with me, saying, 'Come up here, and I will show you things which must take place after this.'"* This is the door of revelation. You need revelation—not just about who Jesus is, but about things to come so that you can maintain a focus on your destiny and learn how to use your authority.

Authority is what it is all about in this hour. God wants you to open the doors to deeper intimacy and revelation so that you will be encouraged to work with Him—to release signs and wonders during a coming revolution of love.

A revolution has begun. Will you be part of it?

The Coming Revolution

I believe that this is the year when God is going to begin to overthrow the religious government—those who have held the true Church of Jesus Christ down. God is going to begin to release a revolution to us. He is going to release the key of David and the key of revelation knowledge, so that there will be a drastic change in ways of thinking and behaving in the Body and even in the nation. And do you know what's going to do it? Love.

Now is the time to do the things that God has put in our hearts. There are so many of you who are full of vision and dreams, but you're wondering when they are ever going to come to pass. Now is the time. The Son of Man is going to open doors that no man can close, and He is going to close doors of hindrance that no one can open.

That's the way it has to be. God is raising up a generation who will have the balance of the Word and the Spirit together. An old revivalist from England, Smith Wigglesworth, once prophesied that the greatest move of God that would happen in the endtimes would be when the Spirit of God marries the Word of God. When the Church moves in signs and wonders, a revival of a billion souls will occur—a revival that cannot be stopped because we move in power and authority. We are in that preseason, when God is calling us to a place of maturity.

I believe that God is about to release a revolution. In a previous chapter, I talked about how God wants to release both the key of love and a revolution to the Body of Christ. I'd like to close the book by bringing more meaning and understanding to what God is doing regarding this love revolution.

Not long ago, the Lord began to speak to me while I was on a prayer walk with Him about the idea of Revolution. One of the ways I really like to enjoy God's presence is to put on my iPod, listen to some good music, and just simply go on a prayer walk with Him. One day, as I was walking near my home in San Diego, California, praying and listening to some music, out of the blue the Lord spoke to me.

He said to me, "Jerame, do you want to know what I am doing in this hour?"

So I said, "Yes, Lord."

He said, "I am about to release a revolution."

"What is that?" I asked.

He replied, "Look up the definition of it in the dictionary, and you will know what I am saying."

So, I went home, but I had no time to look up the word *revolution* immediately because I had to pick up a guest speaker who was flying in for a conference that weekend. Instead, I jumped into the shower and got ready to drive to the airport. As I was getting dressed, I decided to wear a brand new T-shirt I had bought the weekend before while ministering in Grand Rapids, Michigan. The graphic on the front of the shirt was an image of the Lion of Judah, who is Jesus. When I took the shirt out of the bag I noticed that on the back, in huge letters across the shoulders, was the word *revolution*. Immediately, I felt the presence of God and knew that God was saying something. Once I returned home from the airport, I had time to investigate what God was showing me.

First, I looked up the meaning of *revolution* in the dictionary: A revolution is a drastic and far reaching change in ways of thinking and behaving that will affect cultures. A revolution is also defined as "the overthrowing of a government by those who are governed."[1]

After reading this, the Lord began to speak to me some more about revolution.

He said to me, "Jerame, I confirmed the word I spoke to you on your walk by the message on the back of the T-shirt that you bought the weekend before. Don't just pay attention to the word *revolution* written on the back of the shirt; pay attention to what was on the front of that shirt as well."

As He said this, I remembered that on the front of the shirt there was a lion.

Then He said to me, "Tell My people this: 'The Lion of Judah is going to release a revolution to His people. He is going to release a drastic change in ways of thinking and behaving in the Body of Christ and even in the nations regarding the Gospel of the Kingdom. And He is also going to overthrow the religious government in the Church, those who have held the true Church of Jesus Christ down through religion and legalism. He is going to appoint true leaders in the Church who will carry the heart of the Father in order to birth a new wineskin and new wine message that will be founded upon the love of God instead of legalism and the law.'"

The New Wine and Wineskin

After hearing the Lord tell me that He was doing a new thing, birthing a new wine message as well as a new wineskin in the Church regarding the Kingdom of God and His love, I wanted to know more. So I asked Him, "What does this new wineskin and wine look like?

What is the message of the new wine, and what is the wineskin to contain it?"

He told me to study Matthew 9:16-17.

I was very familiar with this passage of Scripture and had read it many times. Jesus tells a parable about the new wine and new wineskins. Let's take a look at this parable. Matthew 9:16-17 reads,

> *No one puts a piece of unshrunk cloth on an old garment; for the patch pulls away from the garment, and the tear is made worse. Nor do they put new wine into old wineskins, or else the wineskins break, the wine is spilled, and the wineskins are ruined. But they put new wine into new wineskins, and both are preserved.*

Despite knowing this Scripture, I began to seek the Lord as to what the new wine and wineskin really meant to Him. I really wanted to know. This was a question that had been in my heart a long time before God began to speak to me about the new wine and wineskin. You see, since I travel all over the world ministering in all kinds of different churches and nations, I had run into a lot of people who were always talking about how they had "the new wine message" and "the new wineskin from Heaven." Most of these people claimed that their ministry or message was the new wine and new wineskin for that hour and that everything else was obsolete, old, and religious. For some reason, I had a hard time with people who claimed that. To me, it almost seemed prideful, as though true revelation only came through one man or woman. No matter how good the message was or how anointed the individual seemed to be, something inside of me knew that there had to be more. In fact, I really struggled with the idea that God would only raise up a few mighty men and women of God to do the things of God, while everyone else just sat and watched. In the Scriptures, I noticed that Jesus would lay His hands on people and send them out. His model was completely different from what I was used to seeing and hearing in most churches around the world.

Then one day, He said to me, "Son, if you really want to understand the new wine message, and the wineskin that contains it, then study the way they made wine in the days of the Bible. Then I will reveal to you what the new wine and wineskin are."

I immediately began to research how wine was made in the days when Jesus walked the earth, and this is what I found out. It was a simple process. In order to make wine back then, people would take fresh grape juice and pour it into a brand-new wineskin, which was made out of dried goatskin. Then they would tie it up on both ends and set it in a cool place for about three months. As time went by, the grape juice would naturally ferment into wine. Eventually, I discovered something very interesting. Once a new wineskin was used for making new wine, it had to be thrown away. If you were to put new wine or grape juice into an old wineskin that had already gone through the fermentation process, the yeast cells that were left behind after the wine is taken out would cause the new wine to ferment at a violent rate that would eventually result in the wineskin popping. Just as Jesus said, *"the wineskins break, the wine is spilled, and the wineskins are ruined"* (Matt. 9:17).

After I studied the way they made wine in the days of Jesus, I asked God, "Now what is the message of the new wine, and what is the new wineskin for Your Kingdom?"

"Jerame, the new wine message is the Gospel of the Kingdom message that Jesus preached when He was in the earth—the message of Heaven invading earth found in Matthew 6:10."

Then, the Lord began to ask me questions. "What was Jesus always concerned about?"

I was a little surprised by that question and replied, "I don't know."

"He was always concerned about someone perverting or watering down the Gospel of the Kingdom message."

All of a sudden, it made sense. Just as the new wine was ruined because of the yeast cells, Jesus warned His disciples about the leaven of the teachings of the Pharisees and religious people of the day (see Matt. 16:12). Jesus told them in Matthew 16:6, *"Beware of the leaven [yeast] of the Pharisees. A little yeast leavens the whole lump."* For the first time, I realized what the new wine message was in the Bible. It was the Gospel of the Kingdom message that Jesus preached everywhere He went (see Matt. 9:35).

In the middle of this revelation, the Father spoke to me again and said, "That's right—you don't get any newer than Jesus."

I realized why I was always so grieved when I would hear people say they had the new wine message and focused on themselves. Jesus was our model in the earth for how to live as sons and daughters of the King. You don't get a newer or better message than what Jesus preached. I still wanted to know more.

So, I asked Him, "What is the wineskin that contains the new wine of this message of the Kingdom?"

Then He said to me something that was so simple. In fact, it kind of shocked me how simple it was.

He said to me, "It's love."

"What do you mean, it's love? That's it?"

Then the Lord explained, "The foundation for everything in My Kingdom is love. There are too many Christians trying to access the realm of Heaven invading the earth without the foundation of love. They are stuck in an Old Testament mind-set. They are trying to receive the new wine of Heaven, this message of the Gospel of the Kingdom power and glory that My son Jesus preached, with an Old Testament mind-set or grid."

All I could do was go, *wow!*

The Lord began to show me that it was His desire that His people would come out of the Old Testament grid and into the new. He showed me that so many believers live their lives and relationship with God out of an Old Testament mind-set. Jesus came to show us a better way (see Heb. 8:6). As I thought more about this concept, I realized it lined right up with the first part of the parable; all these people were trying to attach a new piece of unshrunk cloth onto an old garment. I realized that the new piece of cloth represented a new covenant that Jesus came to bring—a covenant of love. The old garment represented the old covenant and all of its religious practices.

Jesus came to do away with the old covenant. Jesus didn't come to abolish the law; He came to fulfill it. Then He released to us a brand-new law. In John 13:34, Jesus says to His disciples, *"A new commandment I give to you, that you love one another; as I have loved you, that you also love one another."*

When He came, many people did not know how to receive Him because He looked and sounded nothing like the religious leaders of His day. In fact, He came to show us a new way of living and thinking. He came with a message that was not of this world. He came preaching the Gospel of the Kingdom of God, and it was a message of power, glory, and love (see Matt. 6:13). Jesus came to do away with the law, and bring life to us by His Spirit (see Rom. 8:1-6). While the Pharisees were focused on keeping the law and fulfilling the Ten Commandments and the Torah, Jesus came to put the Word of God into action. As the Pharisees were focused on legalistic doctrines and themselves, Jesus went about revealing His Father's love by bringing Heaven to the earth through signs, wonders, and miracles.

You see, it is no different in our time than it was in the days of Jesus.

We need to reveal the Father's love by bringing the things of Heaven to earth—signs, wonders, miracles, healing, and deliverance—tokens of the Father's love.

As you receive encounters with the Lord and deeper revelation of who He is and His ways, you are invited to give them away.

Are you ready to join the revolution of love? The Father is calling you. Come join us. Pick up the keys. Unlock the doors for yourself and for others.

The Key

The key to stepping into the revolution of God's love is to simply hold onto that key of intimacy. If you want to come closer to Jesus, come! Jesus holds the door open to you anytime! Luke 11:10 says, *"For everyone who asks receives; he who seeks finds; and to him who knocks, it will be opened."* Pursue God. He is always holding open the door to relationship with you. And He is always inviting you to ask boldly for what you need, to do what He is calling you to do. Do you need wisdom? Ask, and He will deposit in your brain just the right strategy to shift the situation that puzzles you. Do you need revelation? Ask, and He will send His angel, a dream, or a vision to you to tell you what is to come, or what to do, or where to go.

Opening the Door

Lord, I want to experience Your revolution in my life. Give me Your heart and mind, and let Your thoughts become my thoughts. Release Your love to me and through me! Here I am! Come, Holy Spirit. I need You more and more every day.

Endnote

1. *Merriam-Webster's Collegiate Dictionary,* 11th ed., s.v., "Revolution." (Springfield, MA: Merriam-Webster, Incorporated, 2004).

POSTSCRIPT: A WORD FOR MY GENERATION

I went to a Panda Express to eat lunch with a friend one day. After ordering the food and sliding my tray up to the cashier to pay, the man behind the counter gave me a fortune cookie.

As he did this, I heard the Lord say, "Ask him for another cookie; I have a word for you."

So I asked the guy behind the counter if I could have another cookie, and to my surprise, he did not want to give it to me. He said, "Only one per customer," but since the Lord told me to ask—I wanted my word.

So I asked one more time, "Please can I have another?" Hesitating for a second, the man reluctantly gave me a second cookie.

My friend and I sat down to eat, and I immediately opened my cookie. This is what it said: "A messenger will soon bring good tidings." After I read the fortune, I was shocked. It was like someone put a Scripture in that cookie right out of the Bible. I had never read a fortune cookie like that one before, but the Lord did say He was going to speak to me.

Later that night, I was upstairs in my room praying in the spirit while I worked out. Workout times are not really moments when you expect God to show up, but God is not confined to a church service. In fact, I've been getting a little used to the odd times that spiritual encounters occur.

As I was working out, the power of God came into the room; it's either that, or I did one too many push-ups. Suddenly, I saw a flash out of the corner of my eye, so I turned toward it and saw an angel standing near me. *Boom!* I fell flat on my face.

The angel walked over to me and stared at me for a second. I noticed several different things about him. He was wearing a crown that contained a gem right in the middle. And the gem shifted colors. It appeared red, then blue, then gold, and repeated—red, blue, gold. The gem in his crown kept changing colors as I watched him. Then I noticed that the angel had something in his hands—a long scepter or rod. It was the kind of scepter that a king would have. Just as I noticed it, the angel shoved it right into my belly. It was a moment of both conception and of birthing when he shoved that rod in my belly. As he did this, I noticed the end of the scepter had an imprint that read, "Jeremiah 1:9." Then I came out of the encounter.

After this experience, my stomach felt like I had done a thousand sit-ups!

Immediately, I went for my Bible. I wanted to see what Jeremiah 1:9-10 was. The scriptural reference was this:

> *Then the Lord put forth His hand and touched my mouth, and the Lord said to me: "Behold, I have put My words in your mouth. See, I have this day set you over the nations and over the kingdoms, to root out and to pull down, to destroy and to throw down, to build and to plant."*

After I read the Scripture, the Lord spoke to me, "Jerame, now is the time that I am going to put My word in your generation's mouth. I'm going to give them authority to be My voice in the nations. They will be those who will root out, pull down, and destroy the devil's kingdom. And they will effectively build, plant, and establish My Kingdom rule and reign in the earth. The way they are going to do it is through the color of the gems you saw on the angel's crown."

Then I remembered the gemstone of shifting colors that was in the middle of the angel's crown. The Lord began to explain the meaning of the colors of the gemstones to me: "The red one represents the manifold wisdom of God; the blue one represents the revelation knowledge of Jesus as Lord and Savior; and the gold one represents the glory of God."

He told that as His people would begin to speak out boldly what He said to them, He would release the manifold wisdom of God, (the red stone) which would root out, pull down, and destroy the powers, principalities, and rulers of the air. After those words accomplished the rooting out of the devil's kingdom, He would then release the blue stone, which is the revelation knowledge of Jesus Christ as Lord and Savior, in order to begin to plant and build a solid foundation of His Kingdom. Finally, the glory (the gold stone) of the Lord would be established in the earth and in the nations.

The Lord continued, "Jerame, I am about to raise up revivalists all over the world who are going to bring the Gospel with authority and with power, and they're going to take it to the nations."

Then the Lord began to give me some personal promises. He said to me, "Jerame, as a sign to you that this is the word of the Lord and My words to you are true, I am going to open up bigger doors for you to be a voice for Me in the nations and win souls. I am going to give you a bigger platform in nations in this season. This will be a sign to you that this is the word of the Lord for your generation."

The day following that encounter, I woke up and checked my voicemail, and on my phone was a message from someone at Toronto Airport Christian fellowship calling on behalf of John Arnott. (John Arnott pastored the church that hosted one of the largest revivals of this century beginning in 1992—known as the Toronto Blessing.) They had called to see if I could take his place in a large crusade in Brazil that month. I called them back, and I was told that the crusade organizers were expecting 20,000 to 30,000 people to show up in these meetings. So I ended up going on his behalf, and God confirmed His word to me within a twenty-four-hour period of time that, indeed, bigger platforms were opening up to my generation.

Whenever we have encounters with the heavenly realm, there should always be good fruit as a result. God immediately confirmed that His word to me was a true word for our generation. I believe that God is beginning to raise up an army to carry His voice in the earth right now. He is going to put His words in our mouths and His power in our hands. In fact, I believe that this generation that God is raising up is you. It's time to begin to seek the face of God and grab hold of the scepter of wisdom, revelation, and glory that the Lord is releasing in this hour.

God is not wasting any time.

He wants our hearts.

I believe that, as a Body, we are in an Exodus 3:1-5 moment. This is where Moses is having a burning bush encounter with God. In Exodus 3:3, Moses decides to turn aside to see the great sight of the burning bush. As he turns aside, he gets the attention of God, and for the first time ever, he hears the voice of his Father (see Exod. 3:4). Then the Lord begins to speak to Moses about his destiny and future. God tells him that he is going to use him mightily to bring all of the Hebrews out of slavery and into freedom. As God is sharing this with Moses, Moses begins to doubt and says to God, *"How are people going to know that You have sent me?"* God replies, *"What is that in your hand?"* (see Exod. 4:1-2). Then Moses declares, "A rod." The Lord tells Moses to cast the rod onto the ground. When he does, the rod becomes a snake, and he runs from it. Then the Lord tells him to pick it back up.

This is where I believe that we are at today. The Lord wants His people to stop running from the supernatural authority that He has given them, and begin to take their rightful inheritance and run with it. Why was Moses afraid of the rod that turned into the snake? He grew up in the courts of Pharaoh, and the only people that Moses had ever seen do supernatural feats were the magicians, witch doctors, witches, or sorcerers of that day. As Moses is freaking out about his rod becoming a snake, God says to him, "Take it by the tail." As he does this, the snake became a rod again in his hand. I believe that this is where we are at as a generation because God wants us as His people to quit running from the supernatural authority that He has given us; instead, we are to receive it and walk in it. So many people are afraid of the supernatural because they have only seen the demonic move in supernatural feats.

After God says to Moses, "Pick that rod up, son," Moses overcomes his fear of the supernatural and the dark side. Then God tells him to go to Pharaoh and demonstrate His signs and wonders. All of a sudden, Moses goes from this guy who doesn't know God to a guy who has an encounter with God's fire, and discovers his destiny. He gains the boldness to go to Pharaoh to whom God says, "Now let My people go." When Pharaoh says, "Show me a miracle," God tells Moses to throw the rod down. Moses throws the rod down, and it becomes a snake. Then Pharaoh calls his guys out: they throw their rods down, and they become snakes as well. It looks like Moses doesn't have anything special by comparison, but then something awesome happens. Moses' rod swallows up all the magicians' rods, and God's power prevails.

Just as with Moses, God wants our generation to embrace what He is doing in this hour and become who He has called us to be. God wants us to turn aside and see what He is doing. Also He wants us to experience the fire of God and embrace the rod of God. For me, I had to turn aside and see the angel and experience the rod of authority going into my belly. As we turn aside to God and receive that fire, everything lines up in our lives. Suddenly, we know how to use the keys of the Kingdom to open doors to the supernatural rule and reign of God and walk in the authority to win souls and take nations.

God wants us to accept our inheritance today. He wants us to take the rod of authority that Jesus gave to us. He said, *"I give you the authority to trample on serpents and scorpions, and over all the power of the enemy, and nothing shall by any means hurt you"* (Luke 10:19).

I believe that God wants to breathe destiny on you. I believe God wants to release you to move into your inheritance as a son and a daughter and take your place in the Kingdom. In fact, He wants you to pick up your rod of authority and step out to the places where He sends you.

I want you to hold that rod up right now—this rod being a rod of power and miracles, a rod of intimacy, a rod of encounter. Symbolically, wherever you are, as an act of faith, lift up the rod of authority and declare that you will be one who steps out in faith to release the power of His authority.

Now I want you to understand a little something about the color of the gems that speak of the authority that Jesus wants you to walk in.

Red: the wisdom of God, the manifold wisdom of God to the powers and principalities, the rulers of the air. You need to seek God for wisdom.

Blue: the revelation of Jesus Christ to the nations by the wisdom and revelation. You need to ask God for revelation about who He is to you and to the world. You need to draw closer to Him.

Gold: the glory that will come. You need to ask to see His glory—just as Moses prayed, *"Show me Your glory."* (See Exodus 33:18.) Out of that encounter, you will carry Christ in you, the hope of glory...to the nations.

So, Lord, I pray that You would release the fire of Your presence and the rod of Your Kingdom upon Your people. Lord, loose wisdom, revelation, and Your glory upon them now! Lord, raise up an army of laid-down lovers who will manifest Your Kingdom to a dying and lost world, and carry Your glory to the nations. Raise up true revivalists who walk in the fullness of their supernatural inheritance. In Jesus' name! Amen.

More About Jerame Nelson

Living At His Feet Ministries

591 Telegraph Canyon Rd. Suite 705
Chula Vista, CA 91910

Website: www.livingathisfeet.org

DESTINY IMAGE PUBLISHERS, INC.

*"Speaking to the Purposes of God for This Generation
and for the Generations to Come."*

VISIT OUR NEW SITE HOME AT
WWW.DESTINYIMAGE.COM

FREE SUBSCRIPTION TO DI NEWSLETTER

Receive free unpublished articles by top DI authors, exclusive
discounts, and free downloads from our best and newest books.

Visit www.destinyimage.com to subscribe.

Write to: Destiny Image
              P.O. Box 310
              Shippensburg, PA 17257-0310

Call: 1-800-722-6774

Email: orders@destinyimage.com

For a complete list of our titles or to place an order
online, visit www.destinyimage.com.

FIND US ON FACEBOOK OR FOLLOW US ON TWITTER.

www.facebook.com/destinyimage   facebook
www.twitter.com/destinyimage   twitter